WESTMAR COLLEGE LIBRARY
LE MARS, IOWA

P9-CPZ-681

AMERICAN EDUCATION
AND RELIGION:
The Problem of Religion in the Schools

RELIGION AND CIVILIZATION SERIES

THE COMMUNICATION OF IDEAS
Lyman Bryson, *Editor*

SPIRITUAL PROBLEMS IN CONTEMPORARY LITERATURE
Stanley Romaine Hopper, *Editor*

RELIGION AND THE WORLD ORDER

WORLD ORDER: ITS INTELLECTUAL AND CULTURAL FOUNDATIONS

FOUNDATIONS OF DEMOCRACY

WELLSPRINGS OF THE AMERICAN SPIRIT
F. Ernest Johnson, *Editor*

GROUP RELATIONS AND GROUP ANTAGONISMS

CIVILIZATION AND GROUP RELATIONSHIPS

UNITY AND DIFFERENCE IN AMERICAN LIFE

DISCRIMINATION AND NATIONAL WELFARE

GREAT EXPRESSIONS OF HUMAN RIGHTS

CONFLICT OF LOYALTIES
R. M. MacIver, *Editor*

LABOR'S RELATION TO CHURCH AND COMMUNITY
Liston Pope, *Editor*

GENERAL EDITORIAL BOARD

Louis Finkelstein

F. Ernest Johnson   R. M. MacIver

George N. Shuster

RELIGION AND CIVILIZATION SERIES

AMERICAN EDUCATION AND RELIGION:

The Problem of Religion in the Schools

A series of addresses

EDITED BY

F. Ernest Johnson

**PROFESSOR EMERITUS OF EDUCATION, TEACHERS
COLLEGE, COLUMBIA UNIVERSITY**

26477

Published by

The INSTITUTE for RELIGIOUS and SOCIAL STUDIES

Distributed by

HARPER & BROTHERS

NEW YORK AND LONDON

2 2 681

LC
111
.I58

COPYRIGHT, 1952
By The Institute for Religious and Social Studies

*All rights reserved including the right
of reproduction in whole or in part
in any form.*

PRINTED IN THE UNITED STATES OF AMERICA
BY THE VAIL-BALLOU PRESS, INC., BINGHAMTON, N. Y.

399.1
I58a

This volume is based on lectures given at The Institute for Religious and Social Studies of The Jewish Theological Seminary of America during the winter of 1950–1951.

Each chapter in this volume represents solely the individual opinion of the author. Neither the Institute nor the editor assumes responsibility for the views expressed. The contributors were invited to address the Institute because of the special contribution each could make to general knowledge of the subject.

3-19-53   Direct   133

DEDICATED TO

THE LEADERS OF AMERICAN EDUCATION,

PROFESSIONAL AND LAY

WHO HAVE BOTH THE RIGHT AND THE
RESPONSIBILITY TO WORK OUT THE
PROBLEM DISCUSSED IN THIS BOOK

FOREWORD

The Institute for Religious and Social Studies was established in The Jewish Theological Seminary of America in 1938. Its purpose is to enable ministers of all faiths to study under the guidance of scholars in various fields, representing different religious groups.

As has been true of the contents of other volumes published by the Institute, there is a considerable variety in these addresses with respect to form and to length. This is due to the varying degrees of formality in the presentation, and to the fact that in some instances a portion of the period was given to discussion.

In preparing the addresses for publication we have been somewhat embarrassed by the fact that since the series was completed a number of events have occurred that should be taken account of in any adequate treatment of the problem with which the addresses are concerned. Most notable of these developments was the publicizing in the spring of 1951 of the report by the Educational Policies Commission, *Moral and Spiritual Values in the Public Schools*. This document has significantly altered the setting in which the issue herein presented has to be discussed.

Also, shortly before the book was to go to press, the United States Supreme Court handed down its decision in the Zorach case, which arose as a test of the constitutionality of New York City's released-time plan of weekday religious education. The ruling opinion in this case now takes its place alongside the Everson and McCollum cases and considerably alters, from the legal point of view, the situation with which various contributors to this series were dealing.

In order to take account of these and other developments during recent months, the editor has taken the liberty of amending and expanding his concluding address. It is hoped that the discussion thereby acquires an "up-to-dateness" that it would otherwise lack.

The Editor.

May, 1952

CONTENTS

ix

AMERICAN EDUCATION
AND RELIGION:

The Problem of Religion in the Schools

I

STATEMENT OF THE PROBLEM

BY

F. ERNEST JOHNSON, D.D.

Professor Emeritus of Education,
Teachers College, Columbia University

In opening another of our Institute series I should perhaps offer an explanation, if not a frank defense, of the topic I have chosen for this first chapter and for the one with which the series is to conclude. It has seemed to me desirable that the problem which gives rise to the entire series on "American Education and Religion" should be stated, if possible, in a way that will bring all the topics to be discussed within one perspective.

It is probably quite true that no two of the writers would state the problem in the same way. Nor would any two, presumably, discuss it within quite the same frame of reference. Yet it is my hope that in the analysis I am about to present, sketchy as it must be, the various views later presented will find points of special relevance. Thus it may be possible to avoid the impression, which any kind of symposium is likely to give, of a lack of focus and interrelatedness among the several parts. At the same time, I cannot too strongly emphasize the complete freedom of every contributor to the series to take issue with this initial analysis if he chooses and to go his "own sweet way."

In the closing chapter, entitled, "Summary and Conclusions," I shall attempt to draw the threads together, but to avoid finding any pattern that is not there. At the least, we shall have brought together the fruits of serious and competent study and reflection by persons whose participation I am happy to have secured, concerning one of the most perplexing problems of our day.

It should also be noted that the term, "American education," is used here to denote chiefly what is coming to be known as general education, signifying the educational program that is considered normative for the population as a whole. Broadly defined, it is education for citizenship in the fullest sense of that word. It covers, roughly, the elementary, secondary, and junior college levels, although the entire curriculum of the liberal arts college is now being conceived in terms of general education. It follows that while general education is in its nature no more public than private, the chief reference of the word, "problem," as used in the title of this paper, is to the situation existing in public education. Nevertheless, we are bringing privately supported education within the scope of the series because in terms of the educative process, as distinguished from public policy, the task of relating religion to the other subject matters of general education is essentially the same, whatever the auspices may be. Moreover, while public education by its very magnitude tends to dominate the general education scene through the secondary level, privately supported higher education will presumably be a very potent force in shaping the general education of the future.

Now I am well aware that there are many educators who insist that there is no real "problem" at all; that it is artificially created by religious leaders. But I have put it in our title, with the definite article—*the* problem—because even those who do not recognize any intrinsically problematic situation in the prevailingly secular character of public education in America, must see that an objective problem exists because of conflicting concerns and demands in the community. To put it tritely, we face a condition and not a theory. My own experience in teaching in a graduate school of education has been very illuminating at this point. When we brought up for consideration in a course on educational foundations the question of the place of religion in general education, many regarded it as an intrusion of an extraneous and troublesome subject. It soon appeared, however, that the students themselves regarded the issue as very real. I think those pursuing graduate studies in educational administration were perhaps the first to sense the reality of the problem as presented in typical American communities. For the educator who regards the issue as in itself artificial, who thinks it should not have been raised, may nevertheless find himself deeply entangled in it because of the conflicting opinions and moods in the community he serves. Hence the problem is there to be faced and cannot be ignored.

Nevertheless it seems to me that the place to begin in our analysis is with the view of those who regard the issue over religion in general education as artificial. That position is by no means without substantial support among educators of high standing and marked professional competence. If I am not mistaken, the reluctance on the part of these leaders to take the criticisms of secular education seriously is due to one of three causes.

First, there are educators who are deeply religious and even active church leaders, in whom the suggestion that general education should give some place to religion, arouses nothing but fear. They recall the battles fought in the past over religious liberty and are disturbed by the suggestion that the state has any responsibility whatever in the religious sphere. They are so concerned over the possibility of state interference in religion—especially in the event the state itself may become the instrument of some powerful religious influence—that they give no serious thought to the contention of others that a wholly secular five-days-in-the-week educational program is inadequate and has undesirable consequences.

Secondly, there are educators of undoubted competence and devotion to their tasks who just have no interest in religion, period. Everything that goes by the name of religion leaves them cold. It is not a matter of being anti-religious, any more than tone-deafness is a matter of being anti-musical. They are not hostile to religion; they are simply bored by it. Just as a person may become absorbed in business, in scientific research, or in sports, to the exclusion of other cultural interests, so these educators regard religion as something entirely expendable. I think many more representatives of this group are found in higher education than at the elementary and secondary levels, and more at the secondary than at the elementary level. Their

attitude is typical of contemporary secularism in the common meaning of that word, which I take to be indifference to religion as irrelevant to the main business of living.

I pause here to say that the foregoing statement is intended to be
purely descriptive. Indeed, if I were discussing the matter in a different context I could argue at length that educational leaders, both
professional and lay, come by their indifference to religion quite
honestly: the exposure they have had to religion in the concrete has
not been convincing. But that is beside the point here.

Thirdly, there are educators who have not only high professional
competence, but a great store of idealism, and who feel a deep kin-
ship with religion in its ethical phase, who nevertheless are not *en
rapport* with traditional religion. They resent being called irreligious;
indeed they sometimes contend stoutly that true religion, properly
understood, has nothing to do with dogma. They would identify
it with ethical aspiration and striving, and extract from it everything
that divides people into sectarian groups. Doctrinal matters they
would like to see relegated, at least to the realm of speculative interest.
These idealists often call themselves humanists, though the term
sometimes brings criticism because it has historical connotations that
these modern humanists would not own. They would resolve the
conflict we are concerned with in this series by substituting "spiritual
values" for religion, thus removing the whole question from the
sphere of political controversy.

This is the position that I would call secularism *in a philosophical
sense*. In my judgment it presents the most serious aspect of our
problem, in that it involves much of the intellectual leadership of our
time. For that reason it is particularly important that it be fully understood. And I feel strongly that it is not understood in religious
circles today. Philosophical secularism rests, as I understand it, on a
conviction that the authentic values of religion can all be apprehended
within the dimensions of ethical experience, that there is no special
religious dimension embodying the trans-historical, and that spiritual
values rest upon no "eternal verities" or "cosmic" sanctions. Whatever we may think of this position, it is held by some of the ablest,
most high-minded, and most conscientious men and women of our

time. To inveigh against it as evil, does not seem to weaken it. More-over, there is no more serious challenge to conventional religion than that which comes from members of this secularist group. Often they put the saints to shame because of their social vision, their high courage, and their sacrificial devotion to ideals which the rest of us profess but too often betray.

Having said this, I must add that philosophical secularism should clarify itself, if it would secure the intellectual respect of the religious world.

Secular "humanists" often invite distrust and hostile judgment. Some of them confuse the religious issue by seeking to redefine the word, "religion," in secularist terms, and then slip back into the traditional use of it when demanding that religion be entirely separate from the affairs of state. Their definition makes religion a broadly ethical affair which concerns every phase of life, including politics; but their polemic use of the word makes it sectarian, ritualistic, sacerdotal. Again, some of the most eminent in this group of think-ers become so ardent that they advocate using the vehicle of public education to win acceptance for a philosophy which repudiates all traditional religion, and at the same time declare that the separation of church and state means keeping all religious controversy out of the schools. This anomalous contention invites the charge that those who put it forward are using a constitutional guarantee to facilitate a virtual nullification of it.

Once more, the group of intellectuals of which I am speaking stands, if I may say so, in its own light by reverting to authoritarian arguments when its stock in trade is to be experimental and adven-turous. Men who scorn the appeal to *laissez faire* in economics and to Jeffersonian individualism in politics, appeal to formulas dating from the Republic's infancy as furnishing authoritative guidance in respect to the constantly evolving relations of church and state—and often end up with an absolutist prescription that does gross violence to their experimentalist philosophy. In all this they do far less than justice to what is intrinsically sound in their position.

In calling attention to these ambiguities in the position of some of our educational leaders, I am fully aware that we all fall into

YORK COLLEGE LIBRARY

ambiguities, and that the arguments of religious groups on the church-state question are far from self-consistent. I have been accused of ambiguity in discussing this issue and very likely not without some justification. But I think any disinterested critic would agree that the group which for convenience I am calling the secular humanists, have thus far failed to put their position on the issue here before us in terms sufficiently unequivocal to make an appraisal of it possible. Yet this same group represents something positive and dynamic in our culture, something that the leaders of religion can ignore only at great cost. By the same token, apologists for religion must learn to speak in a language that minds conditioned by scientific disciplines can understand. I am constrained to say that if as a by-product of the current discussion of the place of religion in education mutual understanding is increased between men of goodwill in avowedly religious and avowedly secularist groups, a great net gain will have been realized.

At the risk of seeming to labor the point, I have stressed this encounter between different philosophical outlooks, because I think it is crucial in the context of this discussion. We are in great danger of having an important controversy settled by *tours de force,* by *ad hoc* court decisions and arbitrary administrative rulings. The first requirement for the resolution of controversy in a democratic society would seem to be a clear understanding of what every group concerned believes to be at stake. This means less tactical maneuvering on all sides and more mutual candor; less of artful polemics and more of honest reasoning together. We are all at fault in the failure to lift this issue to the level of mature discussion.

I wish now to offer a general definition of our problem and then to break it down in terms of certain alternatives that present themselves. This is not the moment for choosing between the alternatives, but rather for clarifying them.

The problem, as the average person sees it, I think may be stated thus: How can public education, in accord with its function of putting each generation in possession of its full cultural heritage, do justice to the religious phase of that heritage without doing violence to religious liberty as constitutionally safeguarded in the First Amendment to the American Constitution and in similar provisions in the constitutions of the several States? As just intimated, this breaks down into a number of subsidiary problems. Let us look at them one by one.

First, and most vexing, is the problem of determining what the separation of church and state means. At first blush it may seem that no significant agreement on this question can be reached within such a group as is represented by this audience or by the lecturers in this series. I hope otherwise. I hope we can all agree that the Constitution is a growing instrument, that basic law as well as statutory law undergoes evolution, the stages of which are marked by successive court decisions. Also, that in a democracy the people must always be alert with respect to growing and changing needs which sometimes can be taken account of by changing the basic law. These principles of adaptation seem to be woven into the fabric of our government and are manifest in our history. This means that each generation may have to make a fresh determination how a continuing principle shall be given operational expression. In the matter before us the principle, I suggest, is religious liberty—everybody's religious liberty. It means that no one is to be restrained or constrained in the matter of religion except as may be required by public health and morals. Incidentally, the fact that this exception to complete liberty is generally acknowledged, indicates that in the final analysis the conscience of the community takes precedence, so far as overt acts are concerned, over private right. That is to say, there is no absolute private right even in the matter of religious freedom. Is it too much to hope that on the matters just enumerated there will be a large measure of agreement among us?

As for judicial interpretation, it seems quite evident that even in the face of recent Supreme Court decisions, uncertainty prevails both in the lower courts and in the public mind as to what the separation principle means, in operational terms. The most striking illustration of this is the fact that in the Everson case, involving the furnishing of free transportation for parochial school children, the Supreme Court upheld that practice after having interpreted the First Amendment as prohibiting public aid to any *and all* religious groups in spreading their faith. Many people thought the actual decision contrary to the judicial doctrine laid down. The same question arises over the distinction made earlier by the Court between aiding church schools and aiding the children of those schools through auxiliary services. I mention these matters, which have no direct bearing on the subject of these papers, merely to show how far we are from a comprehensive and definitive rule where the separation doctrine is involved.

From a democratic viewpoint is it not better so? When in 1925 the Supreme Court nullified an Oregon statute which interfered with the right of parents to send their children to a school of their own choosing, an eminent Catholic scholar said to me, "Of course, I am glad to have it decided that way, but I wish the people had corrected the error through their legislature and not left it to the Court to decide." That strikes me as exactly right. It seems to me that the problem we have set ourselves offers a rare opportunity for what may be called a project in adult political education which will attempt to spell out in terms of educational procedure the principle of religious liberty. Can we not all agree that every population group has a stake in public education, that the way in which a widely felt need for religious education is to be met is a concern of the whole community, that no precedents are to be regarded as not subject to review, and that not even the writings of the Founding Fathers are to be looked upon as infallible political scriptures?

I suggest that in this spelling-out process we are likely to find solutions emerging out of concrete situations, a bit at a time, not taking form in full blown doctrines distilled from single cases as has been attempted by some in interpreting the decision, in the McCollum case, which reaffirmed the Everson doctrine in outlawing the released-time plan for religious education in Champaign, Illinois. Let us at least consider the judicial process as a means of discovering equities and testing procedures rather than as a clamping of the lid on social experimentation. Personally, I should like to see a national policy adopted that would permit a wide range of local experimentation, with the courts standing guard and ready to intervene only when there is a "clear and present danger" that some violation of religious liberty will occur.

The second issue I would emphasize in the effort to define alternatives is that of the (ultimate validity of the private school in a democracy.) I have already alluded to the Oregon School Law case, as setting a liberal precedent. But a little reflection will show that in the matter of private schools—and in this context we mean religious day schools—the American attitude is ambivalent. To the best of my knowledge the public reaction to the decision a quarter century ago in the Oregon case was overwhelmingly favorable. Aside from protecting a basic religious liberty, it erected a barrier against a state monopoly of education. Yet the parochial school is widely disapproved among non-Catholics, on the ground that it weakens the public school, which is regarded as the very foundation of American democracy. We want parents to be as free as possible in the choice of schools for their children, yet every indication that parochial schools are growing is taken as an evil portent. We find it difficult to "have it both ways."

I am giving high priority to this question of the parochial school, because from a strictly religious point of view the most logical solution of our problem is a school in which secular and religious elements can be combined in a wholly natural fashion. It is not strange that in the light of recent developments there should be an increase in the number of religious day schools. But obvious difficulties present themselves. Does not education within a select group, in conscious isolation from the main body of one's "peers," operate against the common interest? To which it may be rejoined that if religion is to be taken seriously, it is more basic than any such consideration. Should the community, then, in the name of religious liberty allow a practice that militates against the common school? To all of us who have sent our children to private schools this comes as more than an academic challenge.

Moreover, the question arises whether a plural school system can possibly approximate in standards of excellence a system which has back of it the resources of the community as a whole. Again, such a question may be embarrassing to us professors and ministers who sing the praises of the public schools and send our children to private schools. Then, too, as a Protestant, I am troubled in conscience by the Catholic argument that any handicap placed upon the parochial school is discrimination against the poor who cannot afford to send their children to expensive private schools.

I am putting the issue provocatively, partly because I do not know the answer, and especially because the prevailing tendency to settle the matter out of hand by the utterance of formulas and shibboleths seems to me distressingly immature. It should be clear, I think, that the usual casual disposal of the parochial school—"All right, if they like it; it's a free country. But it's too bad we have to have it"—this facile way of disposing of the matter, indicates a complete failure to see what is involved *either from a religious or an educational point of view*. My strong inclination is to be a partisan of the public school, but I am pretty sure that all those, whether Protestant, Jewish, or secularist, who think they have disposed of the religious day school by treating it as indicating a mere group idiosyncracy, are only confusing the matter. They have utterly failed to see what the problem is.

Thirdly, there emerges the released-time question. This has been discussed so thoroughly since the McCollum case was decided by the Supreme Court in 1948 that we need not spend much time on it here. It should be said, however, that in the long process, which has apparently begun, of clarifying the issue in the courts, there is an excellent opportunity to develop a public opinion on the larger question of which this is a part, namely, what the school's responsibility is in relation to religion. Released time is at best an effort to compensate a defect. It came into existence because people were dissatisfied with a wholly secular education and saw no alternative to providing religious education in this marginal, supplementary fashion. Once more, I hope all of us who are concerned with education can agree that a judicial prohibition is like the damming of a stream: it leaves for future determination where the stream will flow.

In this connection some subordinate but important questions arise. I will mention two. Might it be better to let the community decide what are the legitimate extra-school demands on children's time for religious education and substitute dismissal for release? Many people would, I think, regard this as preferable. If it is felt that some real disadvantage would be incurred, should not the religious educators concerned face squarely the challenge of those who say that what is really sought is the aid of compulsory school attendance laws in securing attendance at religious classes? On the other hand—and this is a basic question of policy—how valid is the complaint that dividing children into groups by religious affiliation or preference makes for the accenting of differences? I am not prepared to answer this question, nor would I care to do so here. But I cannot refrain from pointing out that educators who exalt "cultural pluralism" and glorify differences in the name of democracy have some explaining to do when they object to children being grouped in accord with religious differences. Unless the argument is put more convincingly, it is almost sure to be interpreted merely as evidence that the people who advance it think religious affiliation inconsequential. It strongly suggests that religion is something like skin color, a mere accident to be overlooked. I am unwilling to believe that those who use this argument want it to be so interpreted, but it certainly needs clarification when used by people who insist that democracy glorifies differences and expresses itself in cultural pluralism.

A fourth alternative encountered in the analysis of our problem has only recently come into prominence. I refer to the proposal now being pressed that the public school itself shall become the instrument of definitely theistic teaching; that it undertake to win the allegiance of children and youth to the Judeo-Christian faith, just as it seeks to win allegiance to what is called the democratic faith. It is probably not inaccurate to say that the advocates of this proposal believe that democracy rests ultimately on this religious faith. The position has been formulated by an eminent official group of Protestant educators speaking through the International Council of Religious Education.[1] In 1949, the Council adopted a statement from which I quote the following:

[1] This organization has since become the Division of Christian Education of the National Council of the Churches of Christ in the U.S.A.

Faith in God, the God of the Old and New Testaments, and faith in freemen as His responsible creations have inspired our life and history from the early days of the nation and in its earlier Colonial history. This faith is embodied in our laws, documents, and institutions. Even those who seem on the surface most indifferent to it, acknowledge its sway in their deeper moments, as when confronted with the stark tragedies of life. . . . As far as the school can, in view of the religious diversity of our people, judicial opinions, and our American traditions, we expect it to teach this common religious tradition as the only adequate basis for the life of the school and the personal lives of teachers, students, and citizens in a free and responsible democracy.

More recently the National Council of Independent Schools issued a statement on "The Functions of Secondary Education in the United States" which was put forward as applicable to all secondary education, public or independent. One paragraph reads as follows:

The tradition of American education derives from faith in God, faith in man, and the ideal of the widest educational opportunities for all. The disestablishment of churches was not intended to interfere with the faith of the people of the United States in a Supreme Being. When the country was founded, it was written into law and established in custom that, while there was to be separation between the powers of the state and those of churches, and while each American was to be protected from compulsory worship with any sect or creed, and while the right of any man to dissent according to his conscience was guaranteed, the reliance on God and trust in Him, by any believer, were to be recognized and perpetuated. Thus the source of our ultimate security and unity is an understanding of man's position in relation to eternal reality and participation in the resources of faith. This is the spiritual heritage to which our children are entitled.[2]

My own impression is that the official Protestant statement just quoted sprang from a feeling of amazed frustration at the decision of the Supreme Court in the McCollum case which, temporarily at least, threw the released-time plan into confusion. Here was a plan laboriously worked out, mainly under Protestant auspices but with

---

[2] National Council of Independent Schools, "The Functions of Secondary Education in the United States," *School and Society,* New York, September 23, 1950.

active Catholic support and participation, developed through many years of experimentation, and specifically designed to preserve the separation of church and state as Protestants, its historic champions, understood that doctrine. Even assuming that the decision was just and wise—and there is wide disagreement on the point—it should occasion no wonder that Protestant leaders were dismayed by it and impelled to develop a more positive strategy.

As for the constitutional questions raised by the proposal—and the Protestant group, you will have noted, put in a caveat on this point—these questions have to be answered in any case before a comprehensive policy can be worked out. For us, it seems to me, two basic questions arise in connection with the proposal that tax-supported schools seek to propagate the Judeo-Christian faith.

The first question is whether religious liberty would be impaired thereby, but I do not wish to argue this question here. I do wish, however, to set over against the two statements quoted above two others. One is from the report of the Committee on Religion and Education of the American Council on Education. It was pointed out that any attempt to abstract from the religions a common core and make it a basis of religious instruction is likely to be unsatisfactory to the religious groups concerned.

Furthermore (said the committee) it must be remembered that not only are there many persons who are outside the churches and synagogues but also that there are those who are actively opposed to their teachings. They have their claim on the schools as well as others. To attempt the formulation of a common theology to be used as the basis of instruction in the sense of indoctrination would be bitterly resented by many persons, some of whom are teachers and others of whom are members of boards of education.[3]

The other quotation is from a British publication, since discontinued, the *Christian News-Letter*. Writing about an official report on the teaching of religion and morals in the common schools of England—a very disturbing report—the editor of the *News-Letter* said that even if it were practicable it would be wrong

[3] *The Relation of Religion to Public Education—the Basic Principles*, Committee on Religion and Education, American Council on Education, Washington, D.C., 1947.

for Christians to seek to impose by authority their own views on their fellow-citizens who do not share them. While far more than can be put into words is bound up with belief in God, to enlist the power of the state on behalf of a theistic basis for national education would in the prevailing mental climate only provoke strong reaction. We have witnessed an attempt to impose atheism by force, and we do not like it.

The second question raised by the proposal that substantive religious instruction be given in public schools concerns educational theory. We do not know as much as we should about the way convictions are formed. We do know, however, that in general education and in Protestant religious education—and I think I can safely add, in Jewish education—there has been a definite trend against indoctrination. If it be assumed that this is a mistaken trend, just consider the probable effect on youth in the secondary school of an indoctrinational policy, however gentle or discreet. Would it not defeat its own ends? Many sincerely religious people would raise the same question about compulsory Bible reading or religious observances in the schools.

The implications of this proposal for higher education I will leave it to others to indicate, if they are so disposed. It will have become evident in this discussion that I consider the main focus of our problem to be at the secondary level. Most of what I am saying today is relevant chiefly to that level. For a variety of reasons colleges and universities under public auspices enjoy a measure of freedom with respect to the teaching of religion that seems to bear little relation to prevailing conceptions of the separation of church and state.

It remains to consider the issues arising out of a fifth alternative—the proposal that the public schools should include in their program the study of religious subject matter, not as a special "discipline," but when and as it is encountered in the existing disciplines. In such a plan the religious classics would fall within the field of English and American literature. Church history would be seen to be intertwined with political and social history. Contemporary religious institutions would come within the scope of the social studies. Questions concerning religion intrude themselves into any uninhibited study of science. And so on. The Committee on Religion and Education of the American Council on Education advocates this approach, without indoctrination. The *Christian Century* has defended the central idea editorially.[4] Mr. Justice Jackson, in his widely quoted separate opinion in the McCollum case, strongly intimated that such inclusion of religious subject matter is indispensable to an adequate program of general education. I was surprised recently when I came upon a quotation from the late Dr. George A. Coe, one of the most ardent defenders of the separation of church and state. It was written in 1940. It reads:

Why should the public schools be at all reticent with respect to the religious factor in our culture? Why not include in the study of history an outline of the development of religion as well as of government? Why not make pupils acquainted with the churches in a community as well as with the fire department? Why not open to pupils the contrasts among sects just as the best schools now handle various controversial social questions? Why should not intelligent appreciation of religion be cultivated as well as intelligent appreciation of "our country"? . . . The principle of separation of churches from the taxing power would not be violated thereby, for this principle does not exclude religion but only sectarianism, and a fully democratic handling of religion would be the exact opposite of a sectarian handling of it.[5]

But here, too, difficulties arise in many minds. After all why should not religion be left entirely to the church and synagogue? I suppose it *can* be done. A New England school superintendent told me his school system had solved the religious problem in the teaching of history. "How?" I asked. "By omitting the Reformation," said he. Many people think that the clear intention of the First Amendment, which was drafted by men who entertained a high regard for religion, was that religion should be wholly isolated from the state. To be weighed against this opinion is the contention that the mere omission of religion from a school program that is advertised and defended as a complete preparation for living, is to foster a negative attitude toward religion, which runs counter to the common will.

---

[4] *The Christian Century*, Chicago, April 28, 1948.
[5] George A. Coe, "What Sort of Religion?", in *International Journal of Religious Education*, November, 1950, XVII, 3, p. 13.

For, in spite of their preoccupation with secular pursuits, the American people cannot be said to be indifferent to religion where their children are concerned. I suggest there is food for long, long thought in that observation.

Again, it is contended that religion is too explosive a subject to be studied as other subject matter is studied—objectively and critically. Perhaps the answer to that must be given by the religious leaders who so largely set the stage in the local community for the consideration of religious questions. On the other hand, one may ask whether any planned and competently guided discussion of the religious issues that naturally arise in a high school history class could be as objectionable to religious people as the smothering of religious interest by silence and disregard.

But a serious question of educational theory has been raised concerning this non-directive education—to borrow a descriptive word from contemporary psychiatry. Modern education stresses involvement and commitment. Is study *about* religion really education at all? This is a fair question in the light of present-day educational psychology. Certainly we would not consider it adequate as *religious* education, which I like to think of as the progressive induction of growing persons into the life of a growing religious community. We must all agree that public education in America cannot do that. But before we decide that the public school can contribute nothing to education in religion because it cannot induce commitment, we may well recall that our children study rival political theories, rival economic theories, and alternative scientific hypotheses without being impelled toward commitment to any one of them. I accept the salutary implications of the now famous formula, "learning by doing," but I hope our students do not have to learn about crime conditions that way. And I am more comfortable when I assume that they do not have to learn about atomic energy that way!

The upshot of this attempt to "state the problem" before us is that what has been treated, now by one side, now by the other, as an open-and-shut issue is in reality a many-sided problem concerning which opposing arguments of considerable force can be marshalled. I have, as many of you know, my own convictions on the subject, and I have heard them commended, heatedly opposed, and absurdly misrepresented. But in moderating this series I am subordinating everything else to the effort to see that the case, so to speak, is fairly tried. And you shall be the jury!

II

AN "EXPERIMENTALIST" POSITION

BY

VIVIAN T. THAYER, PH.D.

Formerly Educational Director,
Ethical Culture Schools

A few years ago a conference of educators drawn from public and private institutions of learning met at Del Monte, California, to consider the role of religion in higher education.[1] This conference agreed on several significant items. It approved the introduction of courses on religion in the curriculum of American colleges, public as well as private. It recommended that the administration apply the criterion of "influence in the field of religion" when appraising the value of staff members and in selecting candidates for teaching positions. It suggested that the need of "similar attributes as assets for teachers" be stressed in teacher-training institutions "so as to insure an increasing flow into the schools of young teachers convinced of the validity of a constructive attitude on religious matters." And, in order "to insure the fullest opportunity for participation on the part of the student in religious activities," it urged that educational institutions cooperate "even more closely with the existing agencies and religious organizations of the established churches."

It is clear, I think, that were this program generally adopted it would go far toward transforming both the theory and the practice of church-state relationships in the field of American public educa-

[1] The deliberations and conclusions of this conference are summarized in a pamphlet published in 1942 by the Edward W. Hazen Foundation, Haddam, Connecticut, entitled, *Conversations on Higher Education and Religion.*

tion. Moreover, to the layman, it represents a cleancut and definite program. Nevertheless, in the introduction to a pamphlet printed for the express purpose of publicizing and furthering the recommendations of the conference, it is stated, "No attempt is made to offer a definition of religion. The difficulty of trying to secure a definition mutually acceptable to all . . . is obvious." [2]

This reluctance to define what is meant by religion has certain strategic advantages at the moment, as it enables the proponents of religion in education to stand shoulder to shoulder in the attempt to breach the wall of separation of church and state. But should their efforts succeed, and they gain access to the forbidden garden, this policy of "strategic obfuscation" (if we may purloin a phrase from T. V. Smith) is not likely to remain an unmixed blessing. Conflict is certain to ensue in order to determine to which victor ultimately belongs the spoils.

Perhaps we can avoid this evil if we identify the religious influences now seeking to introduce religion into public education, and the concepts of religion they would further through the schools.

I

First are the traditionalists or dogmatists in religion. Included in this group are both Catholics and Protestants who are convinced that they have a monopoly on truth. Religion so conceived was defined by Justice Fields in *Reynolds v. United States*.[3] Said the Justice, "The term religion has reference to one's views of his relation to his Creator, and to the obligations they impose of reverence for His being and character, and of obedience to His will."

Members of this group agree in identifying religion with belief in an ultimate reality outside the stream of human experience but which defines and dictates the standards for man's proper relation to man. They are not of one mind, however, regarding the attributes of this ultimate reality or the specifics of conduct that come to them

---

[2] *Ibid.*, p. 6.
[3] Reynolds v. United States, 98 U.S. 145 (1878).

as absolute injunctions. Nevertheless, the conviction of each sect that to it alone is entrusted the Truth imposes upon it the obligation to use the schools, directly or indirectly,[4] in order to influence the children of the unfaithful as well as the faithful.

Dogmatists are in agreement further on the proposition that orthodoxy in religion is a necessary condition of moral health and civic well-being. For example, W. S. Fleming, author of *God in Our Public Schools,* warns us that unless the Protestant Bible is returned to the classroom as a book to be read and accepted literally and on faith, our children will grow up "with no knowledge of God and His rules of conduct—practically pagans, potentially dangerous citizens, candidates for the prison cell, without hope in time or eternity." [5]

In a similar voice the Division of Christian Education of the Protestant Council of the City of New York informed the people of New York a few years ago that the 500,000 children of that city who, according to its records, were receiving no religious education, "are a menace to society, to themselves, to our country and our country's future." [6]

These preconceptions are, of course, in harmony with those expressed by the Catholic Bishops in the United States in their *Statement on Education of Children.* According to these authorities, "The continuance and well-being of a State based on democratic principles require that it show a lively concern for moral principles and practices which are firmly grounded only in religion."

On this, then, the dogmatists are agreed: the evil that men do flows inevitably from ignorance of God's nature or from neglect of His injunctions. Consequently, despite irreconcilable differences re-

---

[4] By direct use of the schools, I mean instruction within the classroom; by indirect, using the weight and influence of the schools in order to promote religion, such as, for example, programs of released time. For the purposes of this discussion there is no difference in principle, merely in the degree of pressure exercised.

[5] W. S. Fleming, *God in Our Schools,* The National Reform Association, Pittsburgh, 1944, p. 229.

[6] *Protestantism Unites in Its Christian Education. A Practical Program of Cooperation,* Protestant Council of the City of New York, New York, 1944.

YORK COLLEGE LIBRARY

specting the nature of the Deity and His will, they demand the removal of existing prohibitions upon the teaching of religion in the schools. Specifically, they insist upon either a reversal of the decision of the Supreme Court in the case of *McCollum v. Board of Education, Champaign, Illinois,* or the adoption of an amendment to the Federal Constitution that will nullify this decision. Failing this, or, as some would have it, supplementing the policy of instruction in religion in public schools, is the demand that public funds be used in support of church schools.

I cannot stop to examine in detail the implications of these proposals. I merely point out that were they adopted we should return to the situation that prevailed more than a century ago. To divert public funds from the exclusive use of public schools would seriously undermine and weaken, if it would not destroy, the effectiveness of public education. Equally serious, for a free education, would be a return to religious indoctrination under the auspices of public education. In addition to stimulating once again the sectarian rivalry and bitter competition which induced our fathers to ban sectarian instruction in the schools, it would bring about an intermixture of methods of thinking that are at odds with each other, and thus weaken a discipline which it is the peculiar function and the unique opportunity of public education to develop.

To this I shall return later.

A second group which seeks to restore religious instruction to the schools shares with the first the assumption that belief in God and man's dependence upon Him is an indispensable condition of individual and social morality, but, unlike the dogmatists, its adherents attribute this potency to the elements of faith that are common to Catholics, Protestants, and Jews, rather than in that which distinguishes the one from the other.

Dean Emeritus Luther A. Weigle, of the Yale Divinity School, is an energetic advocate of this position. He believes that "underlying all our differences, America has a common religious faith—common not in the sense that everybody shares it, for there are some among us who deny or ignore God; but in the sense that it is common to the three religious groups—Protestant, Catholic, and Jewish—to which the great majority of American citizens belong." [7] And in 1949, the International Council of Religious Education stated as follows:

Faith in God, the God of the Old and New Testaments, and faith in free men as His responsible creations have inspired our life and history from the early days of the nation and in its earlier Colonial history. . . . As far as the school can, in view of the religious diversity of our people, judicial opinions, and our American traditions, we expect it to teach this common religious tradition as the only adequate basis for the life of the school and the personal lives of teachers, students, and citizens in a free and responsible democracy.

Dean Weigle and others who see eye to eye with him would have pupils in public schools share in the experience of reading from the Bible (presumably from the Protestant Bible), reciting the Lord's Prayer, and receiving instruction designed to instil in them the conviction that morality is, as he says, grounded "in the structure of the Universe and in the nature of God." Evidently Dean Weigle believes with the authors of *The Spiritual Basis of Democracy* (a statement issued in 1942 by seven Princeton professors) that both morality and democracy are grounded in a spiritual conception of life which derives exclusively from the Hebrew-Christian tradition. This being true, the mission of our schools is clear: it is to foster allegiance to Judeo-Christian metaphysics as a common religious faith.

On first view this second group is more urbane and generous in disposition than are the dogmatists; but only on the surface. Consider, for example, the arrogance, or shall we say the parochialism, in the assumption that unless the peoples of the earth become as of one religious orientation, they cannot hope to achieve democracy. Or the spirit of exclusion that brushes aside the religious affiliations of all who are neither Catholics, Jews, nor conventional Protestants. Have their children no rights to be respected in the American public school?

Moreover, the term, "common religious faith," is misleading, for it

[7] Luther A. Weigle, "The American Tradition and the Relation between Religion and Education," *Religion and Public Education, Reports of Committees and Conferences,* American Council on Education Studies, Series I, IX, 22, Washington, D.C., 1945, p. 33.

is common in no more than name. To say that Catholics, Jews, and Protestants agree in worshipping "one God, Creator of all things, and Father of men," neither establishes an identity of point of view respecting the attributes of God nor does it prove that the nature of the father-son relationship implied in the term, "Father," is not without profoundly different implications in idea as well as in practice. If this be doubted, may I ask to what extent would the leaders of the different faiths agree to an arrangement whereby religious instruction were given consistently by the teachers of a faith other than that to which children belong: Catholics being taught by Protestants or Jews, Jews by Protestants or Catholics, Protestants by Catholics or Jews?

Finally, the advocates of a common core of religious instruction, as well as the dogmatists, would do well to contemplate the logic of thinking and the procedures of instruction implied in the words of the Supreme Court of the United States in the case of *West Virginia State Board of Education v. Barnette*. Said the Court, "If there is any fixed star in our constitutional constellation, it is that no official, high or petty, can prescribe what shall be orthodox in politics, nationalism, religion, or other matters of opinion; or force its citizens to confess by word or act their faith therein." [8]

A third group concerned with religion in education is less parochial than the two discussed. In their best moments its adherents would ban all sectarian instruction from the curriculum of the public school. The key to their position is found in a distinction between the structure and the function of religion. By religion as a structure, is meant the specific doctrines, rituals, symbolism, and practices which distinguish one religious faith from another; whereas religion as a function refers to a "quality of behavior" which presumably all religious structures yield, but which it is believed, can be distilled or promoted independently of any one specific faith or creed.

When faced with a practical situation, however, the members of this third group are by no means in agreement as to where the structure of religion leaves off and function begins. Some differ little, if any, from the advocates of a common core of religious content.

[8] West Virginia State Board of Education v. Barnette, 319 U.S. 624 (1943).

Others, as for instance, Dr. Ward Madden, in a paper read before the Philosophy of Education Society in February, 1950, goes so far as to suggest that the concept of religion as a function embraces atheists, as well as religionists. Religion as a function, according to Madden, is identical with the process of evaluation, such as the weighing of one proposed line of conduct against another, the resolving of conflicts between ideals through the reconstruction of ideals, or an appeal to an overarching ideal, or the creation of a new ideal which will guide men as a cloud by day and a pillar of fire by night. Activities of this character, are common to all men; and if the term, "religion," can be applied to them, obviously religious education is an essential ingredient of all good education. Nay, it is the primary function of the school.

The program of this group is democratic with respect to competing religious interests. Democratic, in the sense that they would have the school play no favorites as between religious faiths. The public school, as they see it, should be strictly neutral in matters of religious content, that is, religion as a structure, at one and the same time that it accepts as a sacred obligation the promotion of religion as a function.

Moreover, in its effects upon the schools the distinction between the function of religion and its sectarian content can serve a salutary purpose. In contrast with the claim of the orthodox to absolute and infallible truth, the functionalist recognizes that the best of us, in matters of religious truth, can see only through the glass darkly. Religious concepts, on this assumption, are no longer presented to the young as truths to be accepted without question. They are viewed, rather, as multiple answers to the riddles of existence which men of insight and vision, but, nevertheless, prone to error, have formulated or have tested to their satisfaction; formulations that some people still accept as absolute truth, but which, in the atmosphere of an educational institution, can serve as no more than grist for the religious mill of others.

This third group is likewise cautious in employing the assumption which has so frequently pitted brother against brother, that orthodoxy in religion, or allegiance to an arbitrary faith, is an indispensable condition of morality. Its members are more inclined to accept the maxim which Catherine Drinker Bowen tells us was a favorite of John Adams, namely, that "There was virtue in the world before there was orthodoxy in it."

This tolerance is a first step toward recognizing that morality is not of necessity dependent upon religion; and is, potentially, at least, a strictly human enterprise.

There is, of course, ample evidence to support the conclusion that men of different faiths can accept and live in accordance with identical principles of conduct. Modern communities are replete with instances in which a Buddhist, an orthodox Jew, a Christian, and a Mohammedan; or, a Catholic, a Christian Scientist, and an atheist can live in the same community as neighbors, ply their trades or professions, exchange the products of their labor, share the responsibilities of citizenship; and, by means of this intercourse, become possessed of common ideals and principles and identical codes of conduct. These common standards are obviously more the product of their shared experiences, of their interrelationships, than they are the logical derivatives of their religious differences. Now, in so far as the distinction between the structure and the function of religion helps to emancipate people from the ancient notion that identical beliefs in religion are essential in order to promote common ideals and practices, it contributes significantly to peace on earth and goodwill toward men.

Finally, the distinction between the function and the structure of religion should dispose those who make it to restrict religion in education to the teaching about religion as distinct from the indoctrination of pupils in the content of any one religious faith; or, to adopt the happy phrase of F. Ernest Johnson, to the *study* of religion in contrast with the *teaching* of religion. This implies an attitude of neutrality on the part of the teacher and a spirit of objectivity in the presentation of materials and points of view analogous to that followed in other areas of controversy or extreme variation of opinion.

All of this is to the good. But, unfortunately, in practice, functionalists frequently further the designs of the dogmatists and the ad-

vocates of a common core of religious instruction. This results from
the fact that the distinction between religion as a structure and religion as a function is essentially fictitious. It represents a distinction
in thought, or one useful for discussion, but it is non-existent in the
actual affairs of men. Unlike the experience of Alice in Wonderland,
there can be no grin without the cat. Consequently, just as soon as a
teacher in the classroom attempts to develop the religious attitude
apart from a sectarian content, he tends to revert to viewpoints which
he believes to be inoffensive, or non-sectarian, but which others
quickly label as sectarian.

Nor have all functionalists emancipated themselves from the assumption that morality requires a metaphysical underwriting in
order to hold men's loyalties. Accordingly, they seek to endow purely
ethical principles, or what others conceive to be secular moral ideals,
with a religious or metaphysical sanction and call upon the school
to propagate them as a religious faith.

Take, for example, J. Paul Williams in a recent article entitled,
"The Schoolmen and Religion." Williams states, on the one hand,
"If those who advocate putting religious instruction into public
education are trying simply to get belief in God indoctrinated at
public expense, they deserve but little support in a society dedicated
to religious freedom. . . . There are, of course, important areas in
which religion is private. . . . But there are certain other areas in
which religion must be public, the concern of all, and shared by
all. These areas are the basic ethical propositions on which society
is founded. Unless these ethical principles attain the level of religious convictions, they lack staying power and society is endangered
by every demagogue who manifests the power to awaken religious fervor." Accordingly, Williams proposes that "The public
school must become a veritable temple for the indoctrination of democracy" by promoting "a code compounded of the Bill of Rights,
the Four Freedoms, the ethical portions of the Ten Commandments,
and the resolute determination to follow the will of the majority and
protect the rights of minorities."

Williams would have the schools develop allegiance to democracy
as a religious faith through acts of worship and by means of "open

indoctrination of the faith that the democratic ideal accords with ultimate reality; whether this reality be conceived in naturalistic or supernaturalistic terms. The youth of America," he exclaims, "must be brought to the conviction that democracy is the very Law of Life. . . ." [9]

Underlying Williams's thinking is the familiar assumption that there can be no abiding loyalty to ideals without an assurance of metaphysical infallibility. Hence he proposes that the schools merely substitute one form of dogmatism for another. But were they to adopt this program of indoctrinating American youth in the fanatical notion that democracy, as we conceive it today, expresses the "Law of Life" and "accords with ultimate reality," tragic results might follow. Democracy in its moral, social, and political expressions would become a static ideal at home and a justification for imperialistic ventures abroad. Let us not forget that we live in a world of plural cultures, a world in which any vision of human relationships, however noble and inspiring in itself, becomes highly inflammable once its adherents claim for it an inclusive sway over the hearts and minds of men. In short, to indoctrinate young people in the conviction that their way of life, be it democratic or autocratic, "accords with ultimate reality," is to enslave their minds and to launch them on a crusade to save men's souls by wrecking men's lives.

I conclude that the distinction between the structure and the function of religion, in its application to education, is unsatisfactory and can be dangerous. In plain fact, there is neither a function without a structure nor a structure without a function.

To be sure, the relative importance of function and structure varies with different religions. As John Herman Randall, Jr., points out in *Preface to Philosophy,* by Hocking, Blanshard, Hendel, and Randall, there are some societies in which the social materials of religion are "moral and imaginative or artistic rather than intellectual." In these instances, religion is less a set of beliefs to be accepted as true and more a "way of life" to be pursued. In the Western world, however, and in those countries in which Protestantism has

---

[9] J. Paul Williams, "The Schoolmen and Religion," *School and Society,* LXX, New York, August 13, 1949, pp. 97–100.

been an important influence, the theoretical aspects of religion have consistently loomed large. To quote Randall:

Ever since the Christian gospel, early in its career, began to appeal to men in the ancient Hellenistic world who had come under Greek influence and developed a strong intellectual interest, Christianity has had a marked concern with explanation, with systematizing and organizing its beliefs into a "theology." This concern with theological beliefs increased with the Schoolmen of the later Middle Ages and reached its height in the great Protestant reformers, who insisted that all Christians must hold correct doctrine. They transmitted it to later generations of Protestants, who, partly because they were minimizing external observances and ritual, and partly because they were giving religious expression to a society in which the intellectual urge to understand was very strong, gave a central place to religious beliefs and adequate intellectual interpretations.[10]

This union of religion and theology is, of course, furthered when-ever and wherever religions compete with each other for adherents.

It is this practical situation that our fathers recognized when they instituted the policy of separation of church and state. It is for this reason, too, that our courts have almost uniformly recognized that theology and religion are inseparable; and, on those rare occasions in which they have attempted to distinguish between religion and its sectarian expression, they have, in fact, identified the broader term, "religion," with one of its sectarian manifestations, such as, for example, the Judeo-Christian affirmation.

Our discussion thus far points the moral of defining clearly what is meant by religion when it is proposed to introduce religion in education. Since we live in a world of plural religions, the proposal means the indoctrination of young people in a theology; in some instance a theology narrowly conceived, in others more broadly en-visaged, but a theology, nevertheless. It contemplates an indoctrina-tion in one of the many interpretations of life's meaning and a paro-chial claim upon young people's loyalties. Indeed, it would clarify

[10] William Ernest Hocking, Brand Blanshard, Charles William Hendel, and John Herman Randall, Jr., *Preface to Philosophy,* The Macmillan Company, New York, 1946, pp. 314 f. Used with the permission of The Macmillan Company.

the issue considerably if we were to substitute in all such suggestions the term, "parochial education," for "religious education."

II

I have said we must be clear as to the concept of religion. It is equally imperative that we safeguard the term, "secular education," from the state of opprobrium to which its enemies seek to reduce it.

For example, the Catholic Bishops of America in their *Statement on Secularism* in November, 1949, identified secularism with a naturalistic philosophy, a point of view, as they put it, "that limits itself not to the material in exclusion of the spiritual, but to the here and now in exclusion to man's relation to God here and hereafter." And, evidently, on the principle that he who is not for me is against me, the Bishops charge public education with the sin of promoting secularism as defined.

The attempt to identify secularism and secular education with the philosophy of naturalism is not confined to Catholics. For example, the report on *The Relation of Religion to Public Education* by a committee of the American Council of Education interprets secularism to mean the "separation of religion from life," and while the committee admits that this does not of necessity imply an acceptance of naturalism in philosophy, it does state that secular education tends to create a dualism that is equivalent to a neglect of religion, if not outright hostility to it.

This proneness to identify secular education with the promotion of a naturalistic explanation of man and his nature, is misleading. It is misleading because it ascribes a sectarian purpose to a movement that has as its primary objective the emancipation of men from the limitations of sectarianism and the furthering of common ways of thinking, feeling, and acting together in areas where multiple and sometimes divergent interests impinge upon each other.

It is easy to understand why the dogmatist in religion should oppose naturalism, as the naturalistic concept of man runs counter to his sacred tenets. The naturalist, for example, ascribes to human

nature an essential wholeness of which he believes the supernatural-
ist would deprive man. He posits potentialities in people for creating the good, the true, and the beautiful, as well as evil, out of the
transactions of men, and the good, as he sees it, consists in those
qualities of character and behavior which ease and free these interrelationships. It is in this sense, that he credits man with the creation
of the standards and ideals which give direction to moral behavior.

Here is a faith that conflicts with the tenets of traditional religion.
But, in all fairness, we should recognize it for what it is: an affirmation of faith, a religion, if you will, which entitles it to the right of
competition in the marketplace with all of the privileges and the
limitations that apply to the propagation of other religions.

Naturalism thus represents a sectarian explanation of life and its
meaning. As such it marks itself off clearly from secularism. Secularism, in contrast, is less an "ism" than a method. Secularism represents
an effort to carve out areas of common agreement and common action
as between people whose interests overlap and who disagree vigorously in matters they consider fundamental. Accordingly, secular
education is an education dedicated to the development of disciplined
ways of thinking and living that are designed to further a free
communication between people of varied background and diverse
convictions who live of necessity in a highly sensitive and interdependent world. It is an education that concentrates upon methods of
procedure appropriate to controversial areas such as politics, social
relations, economic life, as well as religion; methods of procedure
that insure a fair hearing for all interested parties and grind the ax
for none.

The secular method merely applies to religion a logic that has
yielded good fruit in other fields. It is a way of thinking and living
which, while not exclusively American, is, nevertheless, a unique
outgrowth of American experience.

Herbert Agar has described this method in his volume, *The Price
of Union*. The price of union, according to Agar, has been the spirit
of accommodation, a willingness of local groups with intense conviction to work hand in hand in the same political party with the
partisans of other interests. This self-discipline, or, if you will, a

disposition to face reality and to accept half a loaf rather than to press for a whole loaf, has welded together a highly diverse people into one nation and has created a spirit of unity and common action in local and regional groups of different interests and, often, conflicting ideologies. To be sure a situation in which, to quote Agar, "a local group might be as extreme as it liked in its own state or district, but when it joined with other groups to act nationally it would leave its radicalism at home," has its obvious dangers; [11] and, unfortunately, American political life has had its bad moments. But opportunism can also be a virtue. According to Walter Lippmann, the habit of opportunism is one of the noblest achievements of democracy, because it testifies to the fact that a people's capacity "to find common ground is stronger than all the many interests that divide it"; and, he adds, "a nation, divided irreconcilably on 'principle,' each party believing it is pure white and the other pitch black, cannot govern itself." [12]

Relations between capital and labor afford a second illustration of this method. As against the doctrine of class conflict which assumes an impassable gulf to separate the interests of economic groups, there has evolved the concept of collective bargaining. Collective bargaining substitutes the conference table for trial by strength. At its best, it insures a fair hearing for all interested parties; thus bringing into clear focus for objective examination the concerns and the needs of all. Secondly, collective bargaining requires a genuine search for ways of resolving differences: perhaps a practical suggestion that promises to insure in some measure a partial satisfaction of the needs represented; or, the reconciliation of sharp edges of disagreement; or, perhaps the formulation of an overarching ideal that disciplines and orders the selfish and exaggerated claims of the various contestants. And, finally, this method involves a willingness to abide by the decision of the conference, to test out in good faith the solution proposed until such time as new conditions require a reassembling around the conference table.

[11] Herbert Agar, *The Price of Union,* Houghton Mifflin Company, Boston, 1950.

[12] Walter Lippmann, "Mr. Churchill and Me-Tooism," *Boston Globe,* January 26, 1950. Quoted in Arthur M. Schlesinger, *The American As Reformer,* Harvard University Press, Cambridge, 1950, p. 53.

In the field of religion and education the spirit of accommodation led first to the establishment of the non-sectarian school, an institution in which Protestants agreed to refrain from inculcating in children the religious tenets on which they disagreed, while continuing to instil doctrines on which they saw eye to eye. Non-sectarianism sowed the seeds of a still more generous concept, and, with the later admission to the school of Catholic and Jewish children, and, finally, of children of still more diverse background, including those of no religious faith at all, non-sectarian education evolved into secular education.

The search for a method of common agreement which characterizes secularism in education, bears both a cause and an effect relation to the principle of separation of church and state. This has as its purpose a freeing of the religious conscience from governmental control. It guarantees to religious organizations and individuals the privilege of formulating and propagating their faiths independently of the state. It takes religion completely out of the sphere of public support and public control; but in exchange for this freedom it imposes the responsibility of self-control and self-support. Religion, in Madison's words, is made "wholly exempt" from the cognizance of civil society.

Secularism is thus a way of thinking which seeks to promote mutual understanding and goodwill in a realm where, as Justice Frankfurter has said, "conflicts are most easily and most bitterly engendered." To repeat, it is in no way identical with naturalism. It is a logic and a discipline by means of which men seek to raise themselves above the battle of religious sects and to succeed at times in alleviating, even reconciling these conflicts; at times in attaining to a vision of a new heaven and a new earth.

III

What are the essential conditions for the development of the secular method in education?

It demands, first of all, a sincere application of the Golden Rule in matters of religious faith. It insists that the devotees of each and all religions respect the religious convictions of their neighbors; that they restrict the applications of their absolutes to themselves alone; that they act upon the principle that what one man accepts as of ultimate validity for himself can be of no more than relative or suggestive value for the religious thinking of another.

Secondly, the secular method requires an abandonment—in its public applications—of the dogma of a necessary connection between religious orthodoxy and morality.

I say the dogma of a *necessary* connection. Just as we find many a sad example of faith without works, so there are abundant instances of men of good works who profess no faith in the conventional sense. Modern society would be in a bad way, indeed, were the good that men do confined to the devotees of traditional religion. To be honest and objective in this matter, we should distinguish, as did William James, between the tender- and the tough-minded individual. For some, the tender-minded, there seems to exist an indispensable relation between a cosmic underwriting of their moral convictions and their practice. Others, the tough-minded, can keep their moral pots boiling on purely human fuel.

The secular method recognizes this difference in people and seeks a *modus vivendi* as between them. It insists merely that what one finds indispensable for himself be not imposed as a condition for the moral education of another.

Finally, the secular method assumes that religion is no exception to the general rule that out of diversity of opinion and free inquiry there emerges, eventually, a truth superior to any one parochial outlook; that the sifting and winnowing process of a sympathetic and understanding consideration of the partial insights of sages and seers is a fruitful preliminary to the formulation of a faith founded upon a rock.

These essential conditions for employing the secular method are not easily realized. They run counter to our human tendency to impose beliefs we hold sacred upon others, and to assume that what we are willing to accept on authority or as self-evident should be equally acceptable to others of goodwill. Secularism forbids no one to follow the logic of conviction in ordering his own life, it merely requires each of us to respect the personality and the integrity of mind of his neighbor.

IV

What, more specifically, does this policy suggest in the program of the school?

Clearly, methods and materials will vary with children of different ages and on different levels of education. In the early years of the elementary school the teacher functions as a substitute parent and the classroom as an enlarged home. A primary essential at this stage is to breed security in the hearts of the young and to further the disposition to deal with the budding new world on friendly terms. To the extent that the home backgrounds of children differ and the religious complexion of the community is varied, the teacher should employ ways and means of furthering both a sense of security in each child with reference to his own religious and cultural background, and a friendly interest in the religious affiliations of his fellows.

On the upper level of the elementary school and in the early years of the secondary school the teacher's role undergoes change. If successful, he now becomes the admired adult in whom the young person is disposed to see, or better, to read the qualities he would make his own. It is the period of hero worship and the crush. Consequently it is highly important that amongst the qualities which the child endeavors to incorporate in his own nature be those of tolerance and the disposition to search out the virtue in points of view and ways of life unlike his own. It is a period in which the school should provide knowledge about religions and, particularly, the religious institutions of the immediate community. Illustrative materials drawn from the world's religions will help young people at this stage to gain an insight into problems acute at their age— parent-child, relations with their peers, etc.—as well as to observe that the common moral and ethical principles have found expression in all religions. This is not the time to introduce courses in comparative religion nor to force upon the young the methods of critical inquiry. Rather is it an age at which to help them acquire a sense of at-homeness in their culture, together with the knowledge and acquaintance of others sufficient to prevent hostility and fear with respect to points of view from which each marks himself off.

While reference materials from the world's religions should be drawn upon generously in these early years, the emphasis should be upon moral rather than religious education as such.

Once the primary and elementary school have given the child a sense of identity with his family, community, and parochial group and a hospitable attitude toward contrasting ways of life, the secondary school can further a pupil's progress toward formulating the faith he will make his own.

It must be stressed, however, that it is the obligation of the classroom to provide merely the raw materials upon which each will work. The school may furnish knowledge about religions as occasion arises in history, literature, social studies, science, etc., and encourage their study; but it is not the function of the public school to determine for the student the faith he should adopt. Young people will readily understand and appreciate the position of the teacher who makes it clear that in matters charged with controversy the task of the instructor is to insure that each contestant for recognition receive equal and exact justice. Encouraged by this example, the student will be disposed to make his own the essentials of democratic practice: fair treatment for opinions conscientiously held, and loyalty to methods of thinking that are public; public in the sense that they employ data and inferences that are open to the examination of all and are designed to widen the area of common agreement without doing violence to legitimate disagreements.

Finally, on the college level, and in some instances prior to college, the school should introduce young people to a scholarly and objective study of comparative religion; a study unhampered in its efforts to promote openminded discussion and to provide the student with the materials of study requisite for free and intelligent inquiry.

Not all communities will permit the teaching of religion in this manner, but in a democracy that aspires to raise up free men, responsible and seasoned in their thinking, it is a goal toward which to strive. In the meantime, and until a community has reached the point where it will permit an objective consideration of religion and not merely promote the religious faiths of dominant sects, there is no alternative to the minimum consideration, if not the exclusion of religion from the curriculum. Certainly, to authorize the use of school time for instruction in religion by its partisans on the ground that the community will not tolerate neutrality and objectivity, or, for the reason that the school is neutral and unbiased, is to sanction an educational procedure we should condemn, were it applied to other areas of disagreement and controversy, such as politics and economics.

In concluding, I should like to refer briefly to the common argument that the authors of the principle of separation of church and state neither envisaged nor could have envisaged a policy of "strict and lofty neutrality as to religion," such as now obtains in American public schools. This argument would have greater force were it not put forth by individuals and groups who use it as an excuse for introducing into the schools their own brand of religion. But, granting the contention, what are its implications?

Certainly it does not justify the absurd charge that the public school is committed to a policy of neutrality akin to, if not identical with, the teaching of atheism. Were we to appeal to the facts, I am convinced that we should find far more classrooms in this country in which teachers, wittingly or unwittingly, are instructing children in sectarian religion than instances in which either the purpose or the practice is "to eliminate God from education."

Nor is it accurate to argue that a policy of neutrality toward religion in public education runs counter to the intentions of our fathers, if, by intentions we mean the spirit which motivated them in contrast with the curricular expression they gave to this spirit in their day. Their basic purpose was to exclude instruction which accentuated religious controversy. Consequently they substituted nonsectarian for sectarian teachings. In so doing they built more wisely than they knew. For them it seemed sufficient to eliminate doctrines that divided Protestants. Later, in a more complex situation, it became evident that this same principle forbade indoctrination in items that set Catholic and Jew apart from Protestants and apart from each other. Today we face a still more complicated situation. Protestants, Catholics, and Jews no longer comprise all of our people, nor do common agreements between them encompass all the religious points of view represented in our population. Consequently, what was non-sectarian yesterday is sectarian today.[13]

The experimentalist takes seriously the existence of religious heterogeneity. He is equally sensitive to the implications of the fact that today no man lives unto himself alone. He asks himself: "How can the younger generation be educated so that men may dwell together in peace in a society characterized by irreducible differences in religion and cultural values as well as an intimate interpenetration of interests?"

For an answer, the experimentalist turns to the secular method of thinking and living, a unique product of American experience in unity and diversity. Secularism, thus interpreted, is neither an "ism" nor a "false philosophy." On the contrary, it is a logic designed to further community of thought and action within an heterogeneous people. It is a logic dedicated to a fair hearing for all points of view with special privileges accorded to none; a method that respects the claims of all contemporary faiths without exception, but senses an equal obligation to faiths as yet unformulated; an obligation to the future which it can discharge only by keeping open the channels of free communication and untrammeled inquiry. It is a method, finally, which has given birth to the American secular school and now relies upon that school for the education of Americans in a way of thinking and a way of life that may well constitute their most distinctive contribution to the creation of one world out of many cultures.

[13] It is this fact, substantially, that the majority of the Supreme Court recognized in the McCollum decision. A careful reading of the majority opinion makes it clear that there is no legal objection, at present, to the *study* of religion in the regular curriculum of the public school. The Court's interdiction applies merely to the use of public school property, public school time, and public school personnel, in order to further the interests of religious organizations.

III

A JEWISH EDUCATOR'S VIEW

BY

SIMON GREENBERG, PH.D.

Vice-Chancellor and Professor of Homiletics,
The Jewish Theological Seminary of America

I grew up in the tradition that in regard to any subject whatsoever any three Jews will have at least four opinions. More recently
this tradition was somewhat modified. Even though my experience
has often contradicted this widely held opinion, I have never been
able to rid myself of it. Hence, whenever I am asked to present the
Jewish attitude on any issue, I am instinctively moved to start with
the statement that there is no such thing as a Jewish attitude, but
only a series of contradictory attitudes held or expressed by different
Jews. I imagine that the committee planning this series of lectures
had this in mind when they asked me to present a "Jewish Educator's View," rather than the Jewish attitude toward the problem
before us. The very title of the paper therefore invites me to express a personal, rather than a group, opinion. However, it seems
to me that this series would not serve its purpose if it did not reach
as far as possible beyond personal attitudes toward group attitudes,
always allowing for the fact that there is no unanimity of opinion
within any group.

To the extent that there is no religious, social, or communal hier-
archy exercising effective authority within the Jewish community,
it is true that there is no identifiable official Jewish attitude on any
subject. But occasionally public discussion, carried on over an extended period in the press and on the platform, results in a consensus

so broadly formulated and widely held that it can with a high degree of justification be referred to as the dominant point of view of the organized and articulate Jewish community.

Such an exceptionally high consensus has been achieved by American Jews on many aspects of the problem of American education and religion. On many aspects of the problem there still exist wide differences of opinion.[1] Before proceeding with my presentation, I shall define the problem as I see it, for the purposes of this paper.

"American education," will refer exclusively to the activities of tax-supported schools. "Religious," will refer not only to the teachings and practices of the presently functioning religious denominations, but also to any kind of metaphysical or theological orientation to life and to the universe.

American education may be related to religion by providing instruction in religion under its own auspices. It may also use its administrative apparatus in a manner that would of necessity compel its students to take a *publicly identifiable position* based on their religious convictions or backgrounds. It is within the scope of this limited definition of our theme that the wide consensus to which we previously referred, exists within the American Jewish community.

We shall proceed, therefore, in the following manner. I. We shall list the various aspects of the problem we intend to discuss. II. We shall indicate the historical, social, and religious factors peculiar to the Jewish community in this country which have a direct bearing on its attitude toward these issues. III. We shall then indicate how these historical and social factors influenced Jewish public opinion on any one specific phase of the over-all problem of religion and public education.

I. *The Various Aspects of our Problem*

Public discussions of the problem of religion and American education repeatedly involve the following questions:

[1] See the *Summary of Joint Conference on Religious Holiday Observances in the Public Schools,* Sponsored Jointly by the Synagogue Council of America and the National Community Relations Advisory Council, held at the Hotel New Yorker, New York City, September 13–14, 1949 (hereafter referred to as *Summary*).

1. *The present curricula of the tax-supported schools.* Are the curricula of our tax-supported schools now adequate to meet all the spiritual and cultural needs of the child as a human being and as a future citizen, so that religious education as such becomes super-fluous or irrelevant? If they are not now thus adequate, can they be made adequate without the introduction of any religious elements?

2. *The privately supported schools.* Are parochial or private schools desirable in principle or acceptable in practice? Should some attendance at the tax-supported school be compulsory for every child?

3. *The legal problem.* What does the First Amendment to the Constitution, which guarantees the freedom of religion and prohibits its establishment in the United States, really mean? What did Jefferson mean, when he spoke of the "wall of separation" between church and state in America?

4. *The non-curricular encroachment of religion upon American education.*

a. What should our attitude be toward Bible readings and toward the celebration of religious festivals in the schools?

b. What should be our attitude toward "released time" or "dismissed time" for religious instruction off or on school premises?

5. *Religion and religious literature as integral parts of courses in history, sociology, and literature.* Shall we introduce the study of religion as a social and a historical phenomenon, and the reading of the Scriptures and other religious classics as part of the schools' courses in history and literature?

II. *The Historical, Social, and Religious Factors Peculiar to the Jewish Community in This Country, which have a Direct Bearing on its Attitude toward the Issues before Us*

1. The experiences of the Jewish people during the past eighteen hundred years of its existence as a minority everywhere, determine more than any other single factor or combination of factors its intuitive, well-nigh instinctive fear of the entrance, in *any* degree, of religion into the required course of studies of the tax-supported

school. Memories and contemporary experiences of active, aggressive missionary activities among Jewish children are too fresh in the mind of the average Jew to prevent visions of a public school system dominated by well-intentioned, zealous religious missionaries, intent upon weaning Jewish children away from the faith of their fathers.

One may with some justice maintain that fear of direct missionary activities among Jewish children while they are within the jurisdiction of the public school is unwarranted. Certainly the law would never permit it. Jews may be oversensitive on the question. But experience has shown that the fear is not altogether groundless.[2] There is a wide gap between any law and its administration. The administrator always has a very wide area within which he can use his own discretion, and that discretion cannot always be depended upon.

Thus, for example, there is no doubt that the law today does not permit sectarian religious services or direct sectarian religious instruction given under school auspices, during regular school hours and on the school premises. Yet in one American community, twenty or thirty per cent of whose population was Jewish, recently during the Christmas season assembly programs were conducted in which priests participated. They intoned the prayers, invoked the Holy Trinity, and Catholic students went out into the aisle to kneel and cross themselves at the proper moments. Moreover, in a number of high schools in that city "speech classes would be assigned the task of spreading the story of the Nativity in sequence form over a period of three weeks, over the public address system, being channelled into every classroom, with priests coming every morning for invoking prayers during the three weeks preceding Christmas day, in which the story of the Nativity was going over the public address systems."[3] If that can happen today when the law specifically prohibits all religious instruction under public school auspices, there may be some ground to fear what might happen, once sectarian instruction came to

---

[2] Thus it was instructive to read in *Information Service,* Department of Research and Education, Federal Council of Churches of Christ in America, New York, October 16, 1943, devoted to the problem of "Religion and Public Education in England," that even within the Christian community in England "bigotry and active proselytism are daily irritants in village life still."

[3] *Summary, op. cit.,* p. 9.

any degree within the purview of the administrative and educational apparatus of the school system.

2. Moreover, the Jew cannot but react unfavorably to any suggestions which would of necessity differentiate his children at stated periods and against their own free will from their fellow students, while they were within the confines or under the auspices of an institution which the law of the land and the exigencies of the situation compel them to attend during a given period of time annually. We know how deeply we all resent the compulsory segregation of citizens in the use of any facility generally open to the public, even though it be privately owned, whether it be a public conveyance, a theater, or a hotel. How much more then does the Jew fear and resent any demarcation between him and his fellow citizens in an institution which his taxes help to support and which offers to his children the opportunities for that minimum education the law compels him to provide for them. The fact that he does not have to join in the singing of Christmas carols in the classroom of the tax-supported school, does not make the average Jewish child comfortable when he is in a classroom the vast majority of whose pupils join lustily in the songs. Even excusing him from class for that period, or permitting him to join a group of Jewish children to sing other songs with them, does not alter the essential fact that while he is under the guidance of a tax-supported institution an act is performed which *of necessity* draws a distinction between him as a Jew and other Americans who are not Jews.

Nor are the religious services offered by the armed forces of America through the chaplains in any way comparable to the situation in the public school system. In the first place, the chaplains are serving mature or presumably mature individuals. Secondly, no denominational services are held at which all must of necessity be present or withdrawal from which is a public act. In the armed forces the religious services are offered under conditions that make their acceptance an absolutely voluntary act on the part of the individual. He takes the necessary steps to join the group at the service. Under public school auspices the individual starts as a member of a group from which he must differentiate himself publicly, if he is determined to vary from the program planned for the group as a whole. Moreover, he is expected to do so while he is still young and therefore very much under the influence of the pressures of public opinion and group psychology.

The sense of real freedom and equality which the Jews have experienced in fullest measure in the tax-supported school of the United States for the first time in their long exilic history, is so precious to them that they fear any proposal which in their opinion may tend even in the slightest degree to introduce into the tax-supported school the thinnest possible line of demarcation between them and their fellow citizens.

That the Jew has reason to be ever on the alert against such differentiations, slight as they may be in the beginning, was amply proved not only by what happened in Western Europe in our day, but by events that occasionally occur even in our hemisphere. Thus a Yiddish newspaper of December 5, 1950, reports an incident in one of the larger communities in Canada. In one of its suburbs Jewish children constituted sixty per cent of the high school population. The local board of education felt that the non-Jewish children were psychologically at a disadvantage when they were in classes in which they were a minority. They therefore ordered that no class should have more than fifty per cent of its members Jews. The surplus Jewish population of the school was then organized into all-Jewish classes. This was proposed and implemented by fine gentlemen, interested in progressive education, and men who would claim freedom from religious or racial bias. But once the principle of differentiation among students on racial or religious grounds is admitted, there is no telling where it can lead. Fortunately this particular error was apparently soon to be rectified. But it required considerable diplomatic maneuvering on the part of the leaders of the Jewish community. Nor can one be certain that the evil of the experiment will be completely eradicated from the memories of the children who participated in it, if only for one term.

This sensitivity to any differentiation between them and the rest of the citizenry in any tax-supported activity of the community, is to my mind unquestionably the most potent conscious and subconscious factor determining the attitude of the Jews toward religion in tax-supported schools.

3. A third factor influencing the Jewish attitude toward introducing religion into the tax-supported school is the content of Jewish religious education as defined by the overwhelming majority of Jewish educators. Jewish religious instruction seeks to transmit to every Jewish child a knowledge of the Hebrew language, of the four thousand years of Jewish history, of the great literary monuments of the traditions, such as the Bible, the Talmud, medieval and modern Hebrew works, and an acquaintance with the current Jewish scene throughout the world. Traditional Jewish religious education never limited itself to instruction in a catechism or in a number of great maxims of morality, or in a limited selection of ethical texts. All attempts to bring religion into the scope of the tax-supported school's interests limit the role of religious instruction to a matter of one period per week. Therefore, the Jewish educator sees very little to gain and very much to lose. A period a week cannot possibly be adequate. Yet it might encourage Jewish parents and children to feel that it is adequate. For every child who might thereby be getting "more than nothing" in religious instruction, another child who might otherwise have followed a fuller curriculum would be encouraged to be satisfied with what seems to most Jewish educators to be a meaningless minimum.

It might be well to digress at this point for a moment from our main outline, and remark that in some communities, at any rate, this "more than nothing" program was found to have more than anticipated value, especially on the high school level.[4] Alert adolescents under proper inspiring leadership can have and have had their appetites whetted for more knowledge as a result of the little knowledge thus gained. But to what extent this appetite is later satisfied is still not subject to empirical evaluation.

4. Finally, Jewish public opinion on this issue is influenced by a very keen sensitivity to the needs and desires of their Protestant and Catholic neighbors. It is with the greatest of hesitation that Jewish

---

[4] Dr. Judah Pilch, when at the head of the Bureau of Jewish Education in Rochester, indicated as much in a private conversation.

religious leaders publicly set themselves against the expressed wishes of so large a segment of Protestant and Catholic leadership which in one form or another seeks to bring religion and the school into more intimate association. This hesitation is due to two causes. The one is an honest concern for their neighbors' understandable and altogether commendable desires. The other is the more crass consideration of self-interest. Jews are made to feel spiritually extremely uncomfortable when they are put in the position of being impediments to what is presented as the needs of the vast majority of the American people for the proper religious education of their youth. On the other hand, Jewish spokesmen have on occasion been told, in no uncertain terms, that their opposition to the programs suggested by Christian leaders for religious instruction within the framework of the tax-supported school may cause an unpleasant eruption of anti-semitic sentiment within church circles. When faced with such warnings, often expressed out of the friendliest of intentions, Jewish spokesmen naturally find it hard to think of the intrinsic merits of the issues. The debate on the question within Jewish circles then passes very often from the level of principle to that of expediency. And on questions of expediency the widest possible differences inevitably arise.

III. *How these Historical and Social Factors Influenced Jewish Public Opinion on the Various Aspects of the Over-all Problem of Religion and Public Education*

1. *The present curricula of the tax-supported schools*

Does American education today meet all the spiritual and cultural needs of the Jewish child? Can it possibly do so? The answer of the Jewish community, as community, to that question is an almost unanimous, NO! The only thinking Jews who give a positive answer to that question are those who are both avowedly anti- or non-religious, and assimilationist in their point of view. Note that these Jews must have both characteristics. They must be both non- or anti-religious, and they must be assimilationists in their outlook on the future of the Jew in America. They must believe that the Jews as an identifiable, self-conscious group should disappear from the American social scene. For there are Jews who are assimilationists without being anti- or non-religious. They desire the elimination of an identifiable Jewish community. But many of them join other religious groups or remain religiously unaffiliated. Their opinions on the question cannot, therefore, be considered as in any way reflective even of a segment of Jewish public opinion. Their opinions are part of the attitude of the religious groups they join, or of that large body of American public opinion made up of the religiously unaffiliated.

But there is also a goodly number of Jews who are anti- or non-religious but not assimilationist. They are secularly minded Jews who want to perpetuate an identifiable Jewish community in this land, but who are concerned only with the preservation of what they call Jewish secular culture. They do not want any kind of religious instruction for their children in or out of the public school. But they do want instruction for their children in Jewish history, in Hebrew, or in Yiddish literature. The most they seek from the American school curriculum is equality of status for Hebrew or Yiddish, as languages, with other foreign languages taught in the school system, and equality of status for Jewish history with the history of other groups of similar size and significance in human affairs. They do not expect that the instruction in these two areas given by the public schools, even under the best of circumstances, would be adequate for their purposes. Hence they seek to establish their own supplementary systems of education. They represent a small minority within the American Jewish community. But they join the majority in agreeing that the present American school system is inadequate for the needs of their children, and in opposing the introduction of religion into the American school in any form whatsoever.

The position of the religiously minded Jew is self-evident. To him, religion and, more specifically, Judaism, is indispensable to the highest levels of the good life. It is the source of his ethical and moral being and sets the goals for his noblest strivings as a human being. As American education today does not provide his child with the opportunities to acquire a thorough knowledge of this religious tradition, it cannot be adequate for him.

Moreover, it is his conviction that American education cannot and should not be so modified as to make it adequate for his needs. It would imply a fundamental revision not only of the school curriculum but of American thought and institutions generally. It would entail of necessity different tax-supported systems of education for different religious groups in America. And for reasons stated above, the average American Jew today believes neither that the present school curriculum is adequate nor that it can or should be made adequate for his religious and cultural needs.

2. *The privately supported schools*

The phenomenon, noted by Dr. F. Ernest Johnson in his opening address of "professors and ministers who sing the praises of the public schools and send their children to private schools," is widely prevalent in Jewish circles as well. The most violent Jewish opponents of Jewish day schools are usually found within the ranks of those who send their own children to private schools. Their opposition is all the more suspect because it is based on the argument of the sanctity of the American public school and its indispensability as the bulwark of American democracy.

It is, however, true that the vast masses of the Jewish people in this country are loyal both in principle and in practice to the public school. Throughout its long history the synagogue never viewed itself as having exclusive, or even primary, authority over the child's education. That authority always rested among Jews with the parents. Nor did the Jewish religious school ever view it as its peculiar province to instruct a child in *all* the knowledge that he needs for his human welfare. Vocational training or secular knowledge was never under exclusively religious sponsorship among Jews.[5] The American Jewish religious day school which teaches French, Latin, geometry, and the sciences, along with Talmud, Bible, and the prayerbook, is by and large a distinctly American product. Such

[5] See my chapter, "Jewish Educational Institutions," in *The Jews: Their History, Culture, and Religion,* edited by Louis Finkelstein, Harper & Brothers, New York, 1949, II, pp. 916 ff.

schools existed among Jews in Eastern Europe before the First World War only in very limited number and because of the very special political and social conditions under which these Jews lived at that time. The schools did not grow out of any theological or religious convictions on the relationship that should exist between the synagogue and the school. Such schools increased rapidly between the two World Wars, as a result of the minority rights which the Jewish communities in Eastern Europe enjoyed under the Versailles treaty. Though Judaism does not obligate the Jews to give their children *all* of their education under Jewish religious auspices, the obvious advantages accruing to religious instruction when it is fully integrated into the total educational process, have led to a very marked increase within the past two decades of Jewish religious day schools in the United States. They still do not reach more than about two per cent of the total Jewish school population in this country. Moreover, because of the tremendous effort required to organize and particularly to maintain such Jewish day schools, no one foresees their continued rapid growth and development. They can never remotely rival the public school in Jewish child population, for they will probably never reach more than eight to ten per cent of the total Jewish school population at any one time. There is no doubt in my mind that if American Jews were told that the American public school system were in real danger of disintegration on account of their day schools, the American Jews, as of today would readily forego their own day schools in order to maintain the public schools.

Whether American Jews would favor a law compelling all children to spend at least part of their student days in public schools, is a question on which I can venture only a guess. I know of no conference or meeting in which this specific question was discussed and a vote taken. My guess is that if the matter should become a public issue, because it became evident that private or parochial schools were threatening the stability of the public school, American Jews if caught off guard might be carried away by their allegiance to the public school, to vote in favor of such a proposal. It would, of course, be a sad day for America if such an issue were ever to become a subject for widespread public discussion directed toward definite political action. The very rise of the issue would indicate a serious deterioration in our social structure.

One thing is certain. American Jews would strongly oppose an absolute government monopoly of education, resulting in the closing of all privately run schools of any kind. Were such an educational monopoly ever to eventuate, it would mark the end of American democracy as we understand it.

3. *The legal problem*

On the legal aspects of the problem of religion and education, the Jewish community naturally tends to agree with those who interpret the Constitution and the American tradition generally in a manner that would make Jefferson's "wall of separation" between church and state taller and wider.

Everyone must agree with Dr. Johnson that in a democratic society "no precedents are to be regarded as not subject to review, and that not even the writings of the Founding Fathers are to be looked upon as infallible political scriptures." [6] We need not assume that the discussions leading to the adoption of the Constitution and the first ten amendments have exhausted all wisdom on the subjects touched upon by these documents. The Founding Fathers themselves wisely recognized that truth. Hence they provided a method for amending the Constitution. But all of us would begin to feel rather uneasy, if certain basic principles of American democracy, such as the right to trial by jury, or of *habeas corpus,* or of freedom of assembly, were suddenly brought into serious question. The present widespread agitation somehow to involve the school in religious instruction, is rightly or wrongly viewed by many as a frontal attack upon one such basic American principle—that of the separation of church and state. It is viewed as being only indirectly a threat to the principle of religious liberty. The two are not identical and they should not be confused. Canadians in the Province of Quebec legally enjoy religious liberty, even though their educational system is both tax-supported and divided along religious lines. Religious liberty is conceivable even when religion is taught directly in tax-supported schools. The separation of church and state is not conceivable under those

[6] Cf. F. Ernest Johnson, "Statement of the Problem," p. 8.

circumstances. Dr. Johnson is of the opinion that there is much that we can do to acquaint the pupils in the public schools with the character and content of religion and its institutions, and with their place in Western civilization generally and within their own communities particularly, without either violating the true import of the principle of the separation of church and state, or endangering the principle of religious liberty.[7] Whether rightly or wrongly, Jews by and large feel that the wall between church and state cannot be made either too high or too wide, because it does have direct bearing upon the principle of religious liberty. The absolute separation of church and state in its Jeffersonian version appears to them to be what the ancient Rabbis would call "a fence"—an additional protection for the principle of religious liberty itself.

Hence, the Jewish community views with suspicion any action that would put tax-collected funds at the service of privately conducted educational agencies. Thus the thing that bothers many about the Everson case in which the Supreme Court declared constitutional the use of tax funds to pay for the transportation of pupils to parochial schools is this: Assuming that there is a public school in the neighborhood of the child, does the state have a right to offer that child transportation facilities out of public funds, in order to enable him to attend a privately conducted school at a distance away from his home? The same problem would, in the opinion of many, not arise in the case of free lunches, because, regardless of where the child studies, he has to eat. But if transportation to a distant point is provided, why not also provide textbooks to the private school for the study of non-religious subject matter? And why not pay out of tax-collected funds for instruction in private schools in non-religious subject matter? The ultimate result that may follow from the impairment of the principle, not of religious liberty, but of separation of church and state, thus takes on rather large and ominous proportions. But I am not now concerned with arguing the merits of the Everson decision, but merely with indicating why the Jewish community would tend to be disturbed by such decisions.

For the same reason, I cannot quite follow Dr. Johnson when he

7 See pp. 14–16.

favors "a national policy . . . that would permit a wide range of local experimentation, with the courts standing guard and ready to intervene only when there is a 'clear and present danger' that some violation of religious liberty will occur." [8] The violations of religious liberty will under ordinary circumstances *not be simultaneous* with the violation of the principle of separation of church and state. Church and state may be united for a long time without affecting religious liberty in any significant manner: witness the situation in England. The two, therefore, must be judged each on its own merit. But the situation in England has its own history. The principle of religious liberty was established in England without the disestablishment of the church. Moreover the church played a much larger role in public education in England until a comparatively recent day than it ever did in America. The development in England until very recently has been toward a constant *contraction* of the role of the church in public education. Our public school system came into being after a long struggle in which its separation from church influence was one of the cardinal issues. For us to open the doors that would permit the church to encroach upon the public school would mean ultimately, I fear, to expose the principle of religious liberty itself to many presently unforeseen but historically experienced dangers.

4. *The non-curricular encroachment of religion upon American education*

a. *Bible Readings and Religious Festivals in the Schools*

Because of the many presently more pressing issues involved in the relationship between religion and public education, the question of Bible readings in the schools has rarely been made the subject of Jewish public discussion in late years. It never disturbed the Jewish community too deeply, because of the slight amount of time involved in the daily Bible reading and the very limited effect this reading has had upon the children. The majority of the teachers responsible for choosing Bible texts to read before their classes usually choose non-controversial passages. Those who in the past chose passages that might offend Jewish religious sensitivities were not

[8] *Ibid.*, pp. 8–9.

sufficiently numerous to stir the community or any section of it into action. As a matter of logical consistency, the official spokesmen of the Jewish community today would most likely agree to eliminate Bible readings also, if it were part of an over-all program to remove all direct religious influences from the school. But, in itself, it represents no vital issue at the moment. Only occasionally, and as the local situation may warrant it, the question of the choice of Bible readings in the schools becomes a matter of concern for the Jewish community.

Jewish leaders have, however, been increasingly disturbed by the encroachment of religion upon the public schools *via* Christmas and Easter celebrations. Reference has already been made to the practices prevalent in some of the high schools in one of the large cities of this country.[9] These practices, on one level of intensity or another, are becoming well-nigh universal. For weeks before Christmas the schools assume a festive atmosphere. Christmas carols are sung, the Christmas story told, enacted, and illustrated. The same is true, but in somewhat lesser degree, of Easter. These celebrations were not part of the public school in its earliest years. When they gradually began to appear, Catholic as well as Jewish religious leaders protested vigorously against them.[10] But these protests were and are of no avail. In addition, these public school celebrations are becoming more rather than less religious in their content and presentation.[11] It is inevitable that it should be so. Christmas and Easter cannot be divorced from their profound religious associations.[12]

In despair of eliminating these observances from the public schools some Jewish leaders proposed the concurrent celebration of Hanukkah and of Passover in the schools where there is a substantial Jewish minority. These joint celebrations were at first accepted with some enthusiasm by Jewish communities. But even a brief period of experimentation convinced the greater majority of Jewish articulate opinion that this course had its grave dangers. Opposition to it has been repeatedly expressed publicly.[13] But on this issue a growing

[9] See above, p. 44.
[10] *Summary, op. cit.*, pp. 15, 16, 17.
[11] *Ibid.*, p. 8.
[12] *Ibid.*, p. 12 f.
[13] *Ibid.*, Appendix A, p. 2.

diversity is evident. The argument in favor of joint Christmas-Hanukkah celebrations is frankly based on considerations of expediency. It runs somewhat as follows: Christmas and Easter celebrations in the public schools are here to stay. Sentiment in their favor is so powerful and widespread that the Jewish community dare not risk the hostility of the majority by continuing to oppose them. Hence let us at least derive whatever good we can out of the situation by introducing wherever possible a Hanukkah or a Passover program.[14]

Many Jewish religious leaders tend to go along with this opportunistic approach for yet another reason. Many Jewish lay leaders and many Jewish parents are strongly opposed to any militant Jewish opposition to Christmas and Easter celebrations in the public school, because they frankly fear that in touching upon such emotionally charged issues, deep anti-Jewish resentments will be stirred within the community. They deem it unwise to rouse the animosity of the majority over a problem that cannot be argued logically. They view it, therefore, as one of the inescapable prices they must pay for being a minority and they look to their schools and homes to counteract whatever negative religious or psychological effects such religious celebrations in the schools may have upon their children. Such sentiments come to the fore in the Jewish press well-nigh annually during the Christmas season, and all too often some Jewish religious leader is rebuked by his constituency for taking too "militant" a stand on this issue.[15]

Judging by what has been happening in the past decade, it appears most likely that the principle of the separation of church and state and, therefore, of the exclusion of religious festivals from the public schools, will be enunciated and defended publicly by Jewish religious leaders, but that the opportunistic policy will be followed as a matter of necessity on the local level. Moreover, this opportunism will be defended on the high ground of intercultural education.

[14] *Ibid.*, p. 16.
[15] See, for example, the article by Dr. S. Margoshes in the Yiddish newspaper, *The Day*, New York, December 23, 1950, and "Happy Chanuka—Merry Christmas," by Shirley Levine in *Opinion*, New York, November–December, 1950.

b. *Released and dismissed time*

The Jewish community in overwhelming majority is unhappy over plans for both released and dismissed time, though dismissed time is more readily accepted as by far the lesser of the two dangers. Nor does it favor the increasing encroachment of the public school upon the child's time, to the point where no time is left for any other educational pursuits. The public school in planning its curricular and extracurricular activities should be cognizant of the fact that it does not and cannot provide for all of the cultural and spiritual needs of the child. It should, therefore, not involve the child in a manner that would make it impossible or extremely difficult for him to attend a supplementary school to receive supplementary instruction over the weekend or during the afternoon hours. The task of occupying the child's time profitably in his after school hours must remain the responsibility of the parents. Agencies functioning during after school hours, established either by the state or by the voluntary association of citizens must be put at the child's disposal for him to use at his own discretion or under the free guidance of his parents.

5. *Religion and religious literature as integral parts of courses in history, sociology and literature*

"It remains to consider the issues arising out of . . . the proposal that the public schools should include in their program the study of religious subject matter, not as a special 'discipline' but when and as it is encountered in the existing disciplines. In such a plan the religious classics would fall within the field of English and American literature. Church history would be seen to be intertwined with political and social history. Contemporary religious institutions would come within the scope of the social studies. Questions concerning religion intrude themselves into any uninhibited study of science. And so on." [16]

This proposal is the one that merits the greatest further study and investigation, because there is an inescapability, an inevitability asso-

---

[16] Cf. Johnson, *op. cit.,* p. 14. See also Dr. F. Ernest Johnson's address on this subject reprinted in *Information Service,* Department of Research and Education, Federal Council of Churches of Christ in America, January 2, 1943.

ciated with it, found in none of the other proposals. The schools cannot be said to be teaching history at all, if they eliminate completely whole areas of vital human experience. Religion and religious institutions have been determining factors in the evolution of civilization. To omit a study of them in a course in history, is to pervert history. The same is true of the relation of the great religious literary monuments to the history of literature generally. Nor can one possibly dodge the religious issue in the teaching of science and philosophy. In those matters it is the public school educator rather than the religious leader who should be the active proponent of the proposal. He should maintain that he perform his task as an educator whose duty it is to evaluate objectively the forces at work in human history, without including the factors of religious institutions and religious literature into his curriculum. It is most unfortunate that so-called secular educators have not spoken up vigorously in behalf of the inclusion of the Bible in a course in literature, and of Church history into the courses in history. But the reason for that is also not far to seek. Religious leaders have refused to permit a consideration of these subjects as part of the general school curriculum except on their own terms. Sufficient thought has not yet been given to the subject, and no significant text has been written that illustrates the manner in which this "inevitable proposal" might be satisfactorily implemented.

On the other hand, its dangers and its pitfalls are patent and numerous. They were vividly brought home to me some years back when my younger son was in his sixth year in public school. He asked me to come to the school one day to watch a pageant on the history of England. He was to be a participant. The school was in a neighborhood ninety-nine per cent of whose residents were Jews. The school population was also ninety-nine per cent Jewish. Of the half-dozen scenes enacted, one was on the introduction of Christianity into England, and my son was chosen to act the part of Augustine. He came on the stage carrying a large cross, followed by a group of Jewish children with crosses in their hands. The effect of this scene on the children who participated in its staging, as well as on the parents and the children in the audience, would have been worth investigating. Obviously this is not the only way in which the history of the Church of England could have been presented. The matter was left to the discretion of a teacher, who to the best of my knowledge was sincere and well-intentioned. But she could have used much more guidance herself.

Conclusion

What then remains to be done of a constructive nature on this matter of religion and public education? Very much indeed.

1. On the college and university level many more opportunities should be offered than there are now for credit courses in religion, its history, literature, doctrines, practices, and institutions.

2. The history of religion and of religious institutions and the literature of religion should be integrated more fully than they now are in the college courses in history, literature, and science.

3. Persistent efforts should be made by religious and non-religious educators to work out texts and syllabi that would indicate how the history of religion and the literature of religion can be integrated into the history and literature courses in the junior and senior years in high school. The attention of the pupil should be drawn especially to the religious elements that are of the very essence of the American democratic tradition, as reflected in such basic documents as the Declaration of Independence, Washington's Farewell Address, Lincoln's Second Inaugural, and in Thanksgiving, the only modern national holiday which has a distinctly religious message.

4. On the elementary and the junior high school levels much more should be done than is now being done to encourage intercultural education, intergroup understanding, and a profounder grasp of the democratic principles upon which America was founded, and to which our country owes its greatest blessings and noblest achievements. Intercultural education and the study of the basic democratic principles embodied in our political institutions, will prepare the pupils for intelligent participation in class discussion on controversial religious matters when they appear in their studies on the higher levels.

5. Religious education in this country must progress to the point

where a human being who has come under its influence will, by
and large, be more easily identified as one whose moral and ethical
conduct is high, who is tolerant and merciful, and who consciously
associates his moral conduct with his religious convictions and practices.

If the ultimate charge against secular education is that it cannot
by its very nature provide the spiritual sustenance indispensable to
sustain high moral standards within a community, then religious
education must give incontrovertible evidence that it is capable of
doing so. I believe it is. But unfortunately this has not yet and for
substantial reasons perhaps may never be established as an incontrovertible, empirically verified fact.

But even if it were so established, that would not, in my opinion,
justify the introduction of direct religious instruction, sectarian or
non-sectarian, within the tax-supported schools and under conditions
that would of necessity differentiate between one student and another.
For the conviction has steadily grown upon me that religion is
contaminated to the degree that it is associated with outer physical
force or with anything even resembling it. If religion is to remain
the matrix for the ethically creative forces residing within or functioning through the human soul, it must be absolutely independent
of the police power of the state. It must represent an energy which
functions under conditions requiring more than the ordinary routine
exertion. It must be the search that leads men beyond the already
achieved and the widely accepted. And government always speaks
for the already achieved and the widely accepted. Just as in philan-
thropy and economics, private initiative must not be crushed or too
greatly discouraged, so in the sphere of education, private, non-gov-
ernmental activity must be enabled to function. It is the most effective measure we can take to prevent the development of a totalitarian
tyrannical society.

Religion, above all, is not served best when it is taught to lean
upon the governmental arm in any way, and society is not served
when its religion becomes too closely identified with its taxing power.
If scientific research on its highest levels has justifiable cause to fear
government encroachment, despite the apparent immediate advan-

tages which may come to it from governmental financial support, how much more wary should religious leaders be in advocating any action that may make religion indebted to the state, and may thus place the heavy and unimaginative hand of government upon that most sensitive core of the human personality, the human soul—as it strives to know and to commune with its Creator!

IV

A CATHOLIC EDUCATOR'S VIEW

BY

RIGHT REVEREND MONSIGNOR FREDERICK G.
HOCHWALT, PH.D.

*Director, Department of Education, National
Catholic Welfare Conference*

I find myself happy to agree with Dr. F. Ernest Johnson in very many of the statements he made in his careful and scholarly analysis of the problem, in the opening chapter. Here and there I disagree with him, but usually I find that this disagreement arises not from a question of fact but more often from the evaluation of a fact, or of its interpretation. It is to be expected, however, that I shall introduce some divergent views with which he may not be in agreement, and with which some of my distinguished associates in this series may even take issue. But such is the nature of the problem. Mindful of Dr. Johnson's expressed hope, I shall try to keep the discussion within focus so that these remarks may be meaningful in terms of the whole question.

I am one with Dr. Johnson in agreeing that the term, "American education," is used here to denote chiefly what is coming to be known as general education, signifying the educational pattern that is considered normative for the population as a whole, and in broad terms constituting what we can rightly call education for citizenship. Again our keynoter demonstrated his mastery over the debated issues in American education, when he so rightly placed the problems of public and private education side by side with the statement that the latter will presumably be a very potent force in shaping the general education of the future. In keeping the problems and the place of private education in proper perspective, Dr. Johnson succeeded in looking at the whole picture, a success that too few educators enjoy for some of them, too many, I fear, would treat the prevalence of private religious schools as a mere group folly which is to be tolerated, or borne manfully by the majority of the population, because of earlier court decisions which they now regard as mistakes that need rectifying.

But if it is difficult for the educational monist to tolerate, for any reason at all, the existence of any kind of school save that which is provided by the state, then it is equally difficult for the American Catholic to face up to the educational realities that lie before him. It is a very real hardship for the Catholic to walk along the paths of democratic living when the shadows of religious disbelief lie so thick across his path that constantly they threaten to trip him up, or at least to endanger the religious belief that he holds to be essential to his way of life. For example, analyze the conflicting attitudes that education alone can give rise to. As a citizen, the Catholic supports public education with his tax dollars, and yet his children, if geography and availability permit, may be in parochial schools, thereby giving him the onerous privilege of contributing to the support of two systems. But the really strange part comes when he finds that because he has exercised a right of conscience to educate his children in a religion-centered school, he seems to have forfeited his right to say anything about public education, and is now looked upon as a separatist, one who endangers national unity, who has given his allegiance to a foreign state, one who has done something un-American. If he shows interest in the election of the public school board, or in the public school curriculum, or in any controversial educational issue, he may be told not to meddle in affairs that are not his—the assumption being that he has now ceded his rights to a voice in public education which has suddenly become something apart from him. All this can happen despite the fact that, depending upon the educational level at which the computation is made, between thirty-two per cent and forty-eight per cent of young Catholic Americans are in public schools. Or take another phase of the problem of education, the problem of religion in public education. Again it is a pretty chancy thing for a Catholic to express opinions in this area. If he suggests that the absence of religion in the curriculum is bad, then he is soundly trounced for having declared the public schools godless, when everyone knows they are the bulwark of democracy; if he suggests that he would like to go along with what was originally a good Protestant idea—released time for religious instruction—he is told that this cannot be, as it is designed apparently as the instrument by which the churches are going to steal the schools away from the teachers; if he objects that the Bible read to students is the King James version, it is suggested that at the very least he is being unreasonably difficult. So you see that the Catholic's conscience can be beset by educational troubles that may complicate his life in the community in which he lives and of which he wants so much to be an integral part.

I would agree wholeheartedly with Dr. Johnson that the issue of secularism in American life is not one that has been raised artificially by religious leaders; rather these leaders have been merely facing up honestly to an issue with which they have been confronted. I find it difficult, however, to be sympathetic with those other religious leaders who are desirous of keeping religion out of education, for if religion is something important enough for them to have dedicated their lives to, it seems important enough to occupy a vital place in the educative process. In fact, it seems to me that such leaders owe an apology to their profession for any attempts they have made to reduce religious education to a side line position. Perhaps Dr. Johnson is right when he says that the educator, who is bored by religion and who considers it expendable, is found in greater numbers in higher education. This has not been my experience, however, for I have found greater interest in religion and a more obviously demonstrated desire to discuss it at the university and college level. Certainly the animus that I have found against religious schools has been more marked at the elementary level than at any other. Denominational and publicly supported colleges through their faculties and student bodies have enjoyed and do enjoy remarkably fine relationships, a condition which is seldom duplicated at the elementary level, where all too often the public school teacher is apt to regard the neighboring century-old religious school as a Johnny-come-lately, an intruder on the scene, or much worse, a competitor for the job of teaching at the elementary level, a competitor that should be eliminated if possible.

The educators who wish to reduce religious education to "spiritual values" that are divorced from doctrinal or dogmatic content are treading on very unsure ground. It is apparent that such a conviction has led its defenders so far from the real definition of religion that some very basic instruction must be undertaken to restore their religious beliefs. Of course, if such persons never believed in the supernatural at all, then a fresh start must be made. But what are we to do about those training centers for ministers or religious teachers which expound, and perhaps unwittingly, philosophical secularism so successfully that some of their star pupils, men of apparent goodwill, are being offered to America as religious leaders, despite the fact that they are men who reject eternal truth and supernatural sanctions.

When Dr. Johnson calls for all apologists of religion to learn to speak in a language that minds conditioned by scientific disciplines can understand, he is making a plea that deserves a full and sympathetic hearing. And yet I would go one step beyond him and suggest to my distinguished friends in science that there is a certain mutuality that ought to be identified here. It seems to me, speaking now from my own experience, that I have gone much further in learning the highly complicated jargon of science than many of my scientific friends have gone in mastering the vocabulary of philosophy and religion. It may sound harsh, yet it is nevertheless true, and I say it regretfully, some of my friends are profoundly competent in scientific research, but at the same time have attainments in philosophy and religion that relegate them to the kindergarten of these fields. In trying to fix a cause for this religious illiteracy, it is impossible to generalize. In some cases no religious instruction was ever attempted; in some other cases, it was resisted when given. Perhaps in still other cases their tutors had little to give except half-truths or misinformation. From my own experience, I know that many of them have never recovered from their early introduction to religion. This is a problem of acute concern to the average Catholic; he must live with his neighbor in charity and in understanding, and consequently it is of paramount importance to him to know what is being said and taught about his own faith. There are times in his life when the thinking Catholic is pretty well convinced that the most subtle kind of attack is being made upon his faith— an attack that aims at the confidence his fellowmen are entitled to have in him as an American who wants to live in peace and security.

Dr. Johnson has stated that the problem is this: How can public education guarantee each generation the possession of its full cultural heritage and still protect religious liberty as we understand it under the American Constitution? But the problem is multiple for the Catholic. He must come to a decision of what is best for the public schools and still preserve the program that is carried on under the auspices of the parochial schools, because he believes in a religion-centered curriculum. For Catholics can never be content merely to cultivate a system whose aim is keyed no higher than to in-tellectual excellence cultivated in a religious atmosphere. This would reduce education to secular training plus the catechism, a system that is highly artificial, to say the least. It is for this reason that Catholics have looked upon a released-time program as an unsatis-factory substitute for the religiously centered curriculum.

In 1944, Edward Leen wrote that, to the Christian, education stands for "that culture of the mind, the will, and the emotions, which, while adapting a man for the exercise of a particular calling, disposes him to achieve an excellent personal and social life within the frame-work of that calling." [1] It is the principal work of the educator, then, to utilize all the means at his disposal, offered by art, science, litera-ture, and revelation to effect this harmony. Leen, and many philoso-phers with him, would put it this way—Christian education is a cultural process by which the reasonable being ushered into this world is prepared, during the years of childhood and adolescence, to play his part worthily as a citizen of the city of men and as a

[1] Edward Leen, *What is Education?*, Sheed & Ward, New York, 1944, pp. 1, 3, and 47.

citizen of the city of God. It is an all-embracing process concerned with the whole man, with his intellect, his will, his emotions, and his physical powers: it aims at securing, by a balanced cultivation and development of all these, that the person may not, in the arena of life, prove a traitor either to his manhood or to his Christianity.

There are certain fundamental truths which the Christian educator must regard as basic to education carried on under religious auspices. They spring from definite truths about man and God, and the relationship between man and God. These principles are: 1. man is a moral being; 2. the voice of conscience is the reflection of the eternal moral law; 3. beyond the revelation in the natural order, God has given a further revelation of divine truth through His Son, Jesus Christ; 4. man is destined for another and more perfect life beyond the grave, for which this life is a preparation.[2] For the Christian, the ideal of character is that set by Christ. This Christian character is based on the supernatural virtues, and the teaching of Christ. The natural virtues are neither neglected nor ignored, but are elevated and sanctified by incorporation within the supernatural ideal. For Catholics, then, moral education without religion fails to measure up to this standard. Moral education alone, devoid of the sanctions and the inspiration of religion, lacks the most vital element for the good life.

It has been pointed out many times that we began our own national life in America with the ringing words of the Northwest Ordinance: "Religion, morality and knowledge being necessary to good government and the happiness of mankind, schools, and the means of education shall be forever encouraged." In those early days, religion, morality, and schooling were almost identical terms.

Today (says Dr. Edward Fitzpatrick) this is no longer the situation, and the progressive secularization of all life including education, is merely another way to state the fact. In the schools this problem was further complicated by the antagonism of religious groups. Today for the Catholic and for other believers in organized religion the place of religion in education is very simple, very clear, and very definite. Religion, furnish-

[2] John D. Redden, and Francis A. Ryan, *A Catholic Philosophy of Education,* Bruce Publishing Company, Milwaukee, 1942, pp. 200 f.

ing as it does a system of spiritual values of life, and a light, or guide, and a way to its ultimate purpose and destiny, is necessarily the end and objective of education. As theology it gives order to the intellectual content of education. As a philosophy of life it furnishes the guidance and the day-to-day experience of men. It is the one thing needful and it furnishes the sanction—the moral sanction—for all the rest of life. The tragedy of the practical situation is that religion is frequently poorly taught and these spiritual values are not realized.[3]

This last statement of Dr. Fitzpatrick is quite revealing. It indicates that the administrators in religious schools are not satisfied merely to announce that their curriculum is religious or to settle for certain external trappings of religion as a sufficient indication that religion is being successfully taught. But a high goal is not easy to achieve. In the ages of faith there was no dichotomy between belief and practice. Consequently, a synthesis was easier to achieve and religion and life moved along together. Since the disruption of the age of faith educators have had to struggle continuously to keep some kind of balance between religion and the secular subjects. Human nature being what it is, it is quite evident that failure plagued the sometimes awkward attempts to integrate the curriculum around the core of religious training. With the advent of improved methods in curriculum study, in the past twenty-five years, Christian educators have had more success in achieving this integration.

Perhaps the most notable success was enjoyed by Dr. George Johnson and his capable staff of assistants in the Commission on American Citizenship at the Catholic University of America. He had been strongly affected during his graduate days in education by the earlier attempts at integration which were undertaken by his teachers at the University, Dr. Edward Pace, and Dr. Thomas Shields. Their ideas, plus some that he had gathered in other student days in Europe, began to germinate and the results demonstrated themselves in the early 1930's in an experimental curriculum devised for the laboratory school, an experimental elementary school on the campus. The curriculum movement under his direction did not

[3] Edward A. Fitzpatrick, *How to Educate Human Beings,* Bruce Publishing Company, Milwaukee, 1950, p. 54.

really emerge into a full program until 1939 when the Commission
on American Citizenship was launched. Between 1939 and 1948 the
Commission produced a three-volume basic curriculum for elementary schools under the title, *Guiding Growth in Christian Social
Living.* To this curriculum was articulated a series of social studies
readers called the "Faith and Freedom" series. It would be pleasant
to report that the curriculum was an instantaneous success, but this
would not be true. It is now widely used and has been accommodated
to the needs of various regions and dioceses, but its beginnings
were slow and uncertain. Teachers had to be trained to use the
curriculum and many workshops and seminars had to be inaugurated
across the country. This type of experimental work is still being carried on with increasing success, and at long last the professional
educator is able to announce that the Catholic schools are more than
a public school program, plus the teaching of the religious catechism.

What is the basic idea of the George Johnson curriculum? It rests
on the principle that human improvement, the true end of education, is total improvement.[4] The curriculum starts with the assumption that we cannot successfully concentrate on one phase of the
life of the individual to the neglect of other phases, because human
personality is a unitary thing which cannot be dissected or divided.
The soul does not exist apart from the body, but is united to it in a
most intimate and vital manner. Therefore our physical health, our
economic well-being, our social and civic relations, our cultural development, all are bound up in the most intimate manner with our
moral and spiritual progress. To educate the child, then, means to
promote his growth in all these spheres. To neglect any one of them
means to stunt his growth in all.

In his introduction to the curriculum, George Johnson points out
the following basic fact:

It is impossible to be neutral in the matter of religion, for underneath
everything that we think or do lies some religious assumption. The very
conviction that religion can be left out of the curriculum with impunity

[4] Sister Mary Joan, O.P., and Sister Mary Nona, O.P., *Guiding Growth in Christian
Social Living,* under the Supervision of the Right Reverend Monsignor George Johnson,
Catholic University of America Press, Washington, D.C., 1944, p. 4.

assumes tacitly that the things of God are not as essential to human well-being as are the things of the world. Bit by bit, this tacit assumption has become an explicit doctrine with the consequent acceptance of secularism as the basis of American educational philosophy.[5]

The heart of George Johnson's educational theory is found in his statement that religion is too important for human welfare to be treated as a mere accessory to life and living. He thought that even a part-time arrangement for its teaching could never amount to more than a poor palliative. Since religion is of the very warp and woof of life, it must be consequently of the very warp and woof of education. With other Christian educators, George Johnson held that our relationship with God is the basis of every other relationship, and our lives have meaning only in reference to our Creator and to His Divine Will. Everything about us belongs to God and any dualism between God and ourselves is definitely false intellectually and dangerously wrong normally.

We arrive then at George Johnson's definition of education as applicable to circumstances here in the United States. Said he: "The aim of Christian education is to provide those experiences which, with the assistance of divine grace, are best calculated to develop in the young the ideas, the attitudes, and the habits that are demanded for Christlike living in our American democratic society." [6]

Hard upon the heels of this definition George Johnson hastened to explain that as Catholics we find no conflict in the picture of "Christlike living in American democratic society." The American form of government and the ideals that inspire the American way of life not only accord with the principles of Christianity, but apart from them lack any substantial foundation. The national heritage which we wish to teach our children in all its fullness is bound up in its essentials with the teachings of Christ. George Johnson found it hard to understand why any educator could fail to perceive that the Judeo-Christian tradition was not only germane to our society but essential to it as the principle from which it springs.

A summary of the basic curriculum, "Guiding Growth in Christian

[5] *Ibid.*, p. 4.
[6] *Ibid.*, p. 5.

Social Living" has been prepared in chart form for teachers. May I indicate in a short paragraph the content of that chart? Education for Christian Social Living means guiding the child in his development of knowledge, attitudes, and actions concerning his relationship to God, to the Church, to his fellowmen, to his natural surroundings, and to himself. This guidance prepares him to meet and deal with persistent personal and social problems that involve his spiritual life, his physical and mental health, his family life responsibilities, his civic and social responsibilities, and his recreation and leisure-time pursuits. This is accomplished through a continual development of the intellect with the aid of pertinent facts (understandings) in the major fields of human knowledge, and the application of skills basic to intelligent study of a problem or situation involving religion, science, social science, language arts, fine arts, reading, the use of library and other resources, and the use of educational measurement. Besides the continual development of the intellect the curriculum is designed to secure a continual strengthening of the will with the aid of the use of the sources of grace, the Sacraments, prayer and self-denial; the development of Christian principles; the habitual practice of virtue. The goal is, of course, the fullness of the Christian character expressing itself in Christian social living, so that the child who has experienced the curriculum may have achieved physical fitness, economic competency, social virtue, cultural development, and most important of all, moral perfection as a member of the Body of Christ.

In the measure that Christian education reaches these goals, it justifies its existence and enriches our national life. At the same time, it increases the measure of human happiness, for it produces people who have grown up unto the measure of the age and the stature of Christ, and who functioning for Him, "go about doing good."

The curriculum has been tested now for more than ten years. Its effects are yet to be felt along the entire educational ladder, because only now are additional experiments being extended to the secondary level. The work of the curriculum is comparatively unknown even in Catholic circles. I am referring, of course, to knowledge on the part of those who are not professional educators. The curriculum will succeed when it finds a place in all the training centers from which all of our teachers, the brothers, the sisters, the lay people, and the priests emerge. Much remains to be done with this part of the program. As for the general public it must be admitted that no attempt was made to explain the integrated curriculum until the recent publication of a ninety-page pictorial review of the Catholic educational system entitled, *These Young Lives.*[7] But this brochure has had a limited printing and distribution.

The Catholic educator, then, has been busily occupied with two phases of his own problem: the completion and diffusion of a basic school curriculum, and a public relations program to demonstrate that the procedures carried on in Catholic schools are fundamentally and scientifically sound. To these problems he must add those that involve the nature of the public school curriculum and the increasingly secular character of American life.

Our awareness of the problem of the separation of church and state is in some ways akin to that of our concern over the atomic bomb. We know that we have it with us and we all share an uneasiness in the knowledge that we do not know how to handle the problem. Some people are inclined to grow weak and ineffectual in the face of the church-state question. "There isn't anything we can do," they say. "Just consider the present temper of the courts of the land. Almost every question that touches the problem of the relation of religion to education is resolved in a manner displeasing to those who support the religious point of view."

To those who are defeatists about this matter, I would suggest that a great deal remains to be done. It is not necessary to forfeit all religious concerns to the secularist point of view. Now is the time to undertake to change the climate of opinion, not by carping at secularism, but by making religious life as dynamic as it can be. If the judiciary suffers today by a prevalence of secularists, then it is time to tighten the educational curriculum and produce idealists who will permit the rights of God to triumph. Ernest Johnson in his keynote paper for this series has rightly pointed out that uncertainty prevails both in the lower courts and in the public mind

[7] Don Sharkey, *These Young Lives,* Sadlier, New York, 1950.

as to what the separation principle means in operational terms. No
such uncertainty, however, characterized the minds of certain religious leaders at the recent White House Conference on Children
in a Democracy. There it was said, and absolutely, that American
law and custom made it impossible for religion to find a place in the
curriculum, and not even at the low place afforded by a released-
time program. If this is to be the tenor for our times, I would in-
voke the opinion of Ernest Johnson that basic law as well as statutory
law undergo evolution, and hope that the evolution to be awaited
will take us in a more satisfactory direction. If "each generation is
to make a fresh determination how a continuing principle shall be
given operational expression," as he says, then I am all for helping
that generation see the light from some vantage point other than that
of the secularist. Here again the remarks of Ernest Johnson are
relevant when he says that the problem of religious education offers
a rare opportunity for what might be called a project in adult
political education which will attempt to spell out in terms of
educational procedure the principle of religious liberty. In the light
of the opinion I am about to offer, Ernest Johnson raises a basic
question when he asks: "Can we not all agree that every population
group has a stake in public education, that the way in which a widely
felt need for religious education is to be met is a concern of the
whole community, that no precedents are to be regarded as not
subject to review, and that not even the writings of the Founding
Fathers are to be looked upon as infallible political scriptures?"

We are to consider, then, the stake that every population group
has in public education, and not to be chained unendingly to precedents or viewpoints. Very well, then let us suggest that *ideally*
speaking, and apart from the inhibitions of custom or legal decisions,
the public schools should serve three interests: first, the interest of
the parents who ought to be allowed to have the kind of school they
want; second, the needs of the community which the school is to
serve; and last, the needs of the state. Please observe that I am not
trying to put words in Ernest Johnson's mouth, nor suggest that
this is his opinion, but I have used his idea as a point of departure,
perhaps. If one agrees with my first point that parents are to be

served, then there would be many kinds of public schools in the United States, each kind serving the needs of parents and the community in which they live. I can sense that some of my listeners are shocked at such a suggestion and are anxious to point out that such a proposal would splinter the public school system into too many small systems, thereby destroying it. My answer is that experience in other countries has not demonstrated that variety of type and kind has in any way hurt or hindered the progress of public education. In some other democratic situations public support of religious education is regarded as necessary to *protect* religious freedom and avoid discriminating against parents who want to give their children a religious education. A long struggle for the rights of private education in Holland has led to very satisfactory conditions there. In fact, the results obtained there in a country of mixed population probably seem incredible to Americans.[8] But it is a situation worthy of study. In Canada, education is controlled partly by the state and partly by the church. This does not mean that there is a Canadian State Church. On the contrary, there is complete separation of church and state, although the two cooperate in certain spheres, such as those of marriage and education.[9] England and Scotland likewise have provided for the choice of parents in education and in doing so have not harmed or hindered the cause of education, nor have they injured the state.

But the secularist will tell you that we can have no such solution in America because they say such a state of affairs "tends to promote divisive tendencies among children." I submit that this slogan is a subterfuge to cloak other reasons for putting an embargo on religious instruction as disruptive of civic unity. Of national unity we must have our share, true enough, but capable political scientists have treated at great length the question of "the general will" and "the will of the people." We have had our good share, too, of champions of "cultural diversity" who have not fallen prey to the plot to straitjacket men's minds for the sake of a secular unity. It has not been

---

[8] Robert C. Hartnett, S.J., editor, *The Right To Educate, A Symposium,* America Press, New York, 1949, p. 5.

[9] *Ibid.,* p. 14.

proved to anyone's satisfaction "that religious diversity erodes the democratic framework of fundamental law whose historic achievement has been to solve the old dilemma of 'the one of the many' by unifying men in political essentials without destroying diversity in social and cultural opportunities, preferences and allegiances— *e pluribus unum*. We have learned that we do not have to destroy plurality for the sake of union." [10] And most of all, we run the risk of stigmatizing as a blemish on American life the very feature of it by which, at this critical hour, it is distinguished from atheistic Communism which now imperils the freedom of mankind.

Political scientists would agree that the threat facing our democracy is one of uniformity and not disunity. Ernest Johnson has asked "how valid is the complaint that dividing children into groups by religious affiliation or preference makes for the accenting of differences?" Father Robert Hartnett follows this question with one of his own, when he seeks a reply to the query: "Where is the evidence that religious education has actually produced 'divisive tendencies' resulting in real damage to our civic unity?" [11] It seems to many of us that the prime discontent over the lack of this so-called unity in American life has come only from the secularist who is even now engaged in enlisting support for a philosophy of secularism which at best has been only partially, and even illogically, formed and offered for consumption to a restless and superficial segment of the American mind.

When I introduced the idea of a public school system that would satisfy the demands of all, I warned that I was speaking only ideally, for it is as obvious to you as it is to me that such a solution has to face almost insurmountable odds. It would have to face the professional school forces who are firmly entrenched, as well as the militant group of secularists who would most certainly seize upon any such move as a prime piece of propaganda and exploit it to the utmost. No, the apostles of religious education cannot engage in any such frontal attack. Before enlisting the secularist in any debate before the conscience of America, religious educators have some

[10] *Ibid.*, p. 46.
[11] *Ibid.*, p. 47.

important homework to do among themselves. Our goals and our methodology have to be more clearly defined, and our teacher training program must be improved to meet the challenge of the times. But perhaps most important of all—religious education has to make unmistakably clear to the American people the traditional as well as the present claim it has upon their loyalties.

One of the first hurdles to be overcome is the fear of indoctrination. If we have something valuable to teach or to say, let us teach or say it. The secularist is busily engaged in selling the idea of secularism. He knows, if we do not, that this is an age that cries for something to cling to. And for the lack of something better, something more appealing, something tangible, many Christian people are taking up the philosophy of secularism, comfortless and cheerless as it is, for want of a better selling program of the way to the kingdom of heaven. I am not saying, as some have said, that what we need is a new Pentecost, but I am suggesting that we could use another St. Paul or two.

In analyzing the problem of religious education in the public school, the special committee of the American Council on Education came to the conclusion that the best that could be hoped for in the public school curriculum was a program that at the very minimum taught about religion, without making any effort to deal with it as such. Not everyone would agree with this solution, and certainly Catholic educators would be divided on the question. Some would agree to the proposal; others would say that the best that could be attempted would be a form of the released- or dismissed-time program. And yet both sides would have to agree that a school program that omits religion and yet is advertised as a complete preparation for living, is in reality giving comfort and consolation to the opposition by fostering a program which runs counter to the traditional will of the country.

In review, what have I said here? I have suggested that there is no clear or easy solution to the problem of religion in education. I have made something of the fact that the Catholic has problems of his own in the perfection of his own religious system, but shares deeply concern with the problem in public schools. I have suggested a solution in the ideal order by proposing anew that we reconsider the basic organization of American public education, if and when this seems legally and constitutionally feasible. But first and foremost I have suggested that this is no time for appeasement in dealing with the secularist mind. The proponents of religious education are in possession of greater reserves than they have mustered for action; it is a time then to reform the ranks and employ some strategy to nullify the divide and conquer techniques of the secularist. I would suggest in closing that the Committee on Religion of the American Council on Education has merely begun its work; if it retires from the field now, religious educators will suffer the loss of one of their most valuable assets. And may I conclude by saying that the sponsors of this series have made a magnificent contribution to American education by seizing upon the opportunity to place the issues before you, for it is you—this audience—and others like you who must make the decision and make it in the best interest of a peaceful and happy nation.

V

A PROTESTANT EDUCATOR'S VIEW

NEVIN C. HARNER, LL.D.

*Professor of Christian Education, Theological
Seminary of the Evangelical and
Reformed Church* [1]

The trepidation with which I approach my assignment in this
series is sufficiently great, but it would be greater still if the title of
this paper were less adroitly phrased. The most likely alternative—
namely, "The Protestant View"—would have set the impossible task
of trying to speak authoritatively for all Protestantism, and this no
one can do. For it is both the glory and weakness of Protestantism that
by its own inherent genius each man is accorded a certain right to
speak for himself, and for himself alone. I am, therefore, grateful for
the less presumptuous and more personal wording, "A Protestant Educator's View." I take it that I am at liberty to voice my own convictions on the matters before us, and I shall not hesitate to do so.
And yet the adjective, "Protestant," contains the warrant for much
more than a personal testimony. We are to examine "American Education and Religion" not chiefly from the standpoint of a sound
philosophy of education, nor yet from a vague orientation of general
theism, but from a distinctively Protestant point of view. It will be
our major endeavor, therefore, to lay bare the essential nature of
Protestantism, and draw therefrom some specific implications for the
problem at hand.

[1] This is one of the last public addresses of Professor Harner, who died on July 24,
1950.

A bit of a preview of the course we plan to pursue may be in order; it may help us to travel the road together. We shall begin by identifying the commonly accepted principles of Protestantism. From these we shall derive some corollaries or middle axioms, which stand halfway between fundamental principles, on the one hand, and a bill of particulars on the other. Finally, we shall deduce a number of practical implications in the area of the mutual relationships of education and religion in America. This lecture, like Gaul of old, is divided into three parts—of equal significance, if not of equal length.

For all its bewildering diversity, Protestantism during the more than four centuries of its existence has rested upon a simple foundation of three easily discernible doctrines: first, the Bible as the source of religious authority; second, the tenet of justification by grace through faith; and, third, the universal priesthood of believers. Philip Schaff, who was first a teacher in my own school and later a member of the faculty of Union Theological Seminary, gave them classical expression in the following words: "There are three fundamental principles of the Reformation: the supremacy of the *Scriptures* over tradition, the supremacy of *faith* over works, and the supremacy of the Christian *people* over an exclusive priesthood. The first may be called the objective, the second the subjective, the third the social or ecclesiastical principle."

This is not the occasion to attempt an exposition of these doctrines, and such an endeavor would not be relevant to our immediate purpose. Suffice it to say, therefore, that the second of the three—namely, justification by grace through faith—is far and away the most important from the standpoint of theology and the religious life. Indeed Reinhold Niebuhr calls it the crucial Reformation doctrine. But, strangely enough, for our present concern we can safely pass it by. If we were trying to formulate a Protestant doctrine of salvation, or shape an adequate Protestant theology, we should have to begin with it, and we might end with it. But it has little enough to do with the problem of American education and religion. For this inquiry we turn our attention to the other two—namely, the Bible as the source of religious authority, and the universal priesthood of believers. These have much to do with the subject before us, and will serve as the underlying presuppositions of everything that follows.

Mounting now to the next story of our house of logic, let us attempt to derive several appropriate corollaries or middle axioms from these two selected Protestant doctrines. If they are true (and Protestantism believes they are and feels obligated to promote them, although it does not insist that others must perforce agree), certain great affirmations follow as inescapably as summer follows spring.

1. *Liberty of conscience for every individual.* From the very beginning these words, in theory if not always in practice, have been a part of the creed of Protestantism. Martin Luther said it clearly in his forthright words: "No one can command or ought to command the soul, except God, Who alone can show it the way to heaven." And the Reformers, as everyone knows, exercised this freedom abundantly. Not only did they make radical changes in church organization, liturgy, and doctrine, but they even approached the Bible itself with a striking independence of soul. In his translation of the German Bible Luther put Hebrews, James, Jude, and Revelation in a separate appendix; and Zwingli did not hesitate to find fault with the book of Revelation.

The inner connection between this affirmation and the essential Protestant principles is not hard to discover. If every man is his own priest, competent to make his own approach to the God of his salvation without the necessary mediation of any other human being, his conscience must be regarded as standing unbound and free. No other view will do! No other conception will prove compatible with the Protestant spirit. Likewise, if the source of authority is the Bible which each believer may read for himself and interpret as he sees fit under the guidance of the Holy Spirit, precisely the same conclusion is reached. The realm of conscience is a holy citadel, which can be overcome from above but which may not be invaded by any person or any institution on its own level of being.

In actual practice Protestantism has not proved to be nearly so atomistic as this affirmation would suggest. As things have worked out, any given individual has more often than not been influenced by the consensus of those who have gone before him, as well as of those who live by his side, and has given deference to the authority of minister, professor, and scholar. As a result we have several hundred denominations, whereas the logic of the situation might imply as many denominations as there are believers. But the root of the matter is still there. The birthright of every Protestant is liberty of conscience under God, subject only to the compulsion of the truth as contained in the Bible and as he is given grace to see it.

2. *Respect for the conscience of another.* This, of course, is merely the obverse of the first-named axiom. If I have the right to make my own approach to God and to seek for myself the truth embodied in the Bible, my neighbor has precisely the same right. He, too, can make his own approach to the same God, and read and study the same Bible. He may return from his excursion into the realm of things invisible having seen something different from what I myself beheld. But who am I to say that he did not see what he claims to have seen? Perhaps he followed a road somewhat different from my own, and the spiritual scenery along the way was not the same as that which greeted my eyes. At all events I must assume it to be so until the contrary is proved, meanwhile testing both his report and my own by all the canons of logic and experience and Biblical truth, and respecting his report as I hope my own will be respected.

Again this affirmation has been a part of Protestantism, in theory at least, from the very start. Martin Luther expressed the judgment that "it is futile and impossible to command, or by force to compel any man's belief." And again the practice of Protestantism has sometimes departed from its theory. There have been Protestant theocracies and state churches from the Geneva of John Calvin to the New England of the Puritans and the established churches of England and Sweden in our own day. In widely varying degrees such regimes have frowned upon dissent and violated the consciences of dissenters. And there are Protestant communions of a confessional type which maintain a rigid creedal standard admitting of no substantial deviation on the part of their membership. But such inconsistencies between theory and practice do not change the essential fact. The true expression of the Protestant genius is a hearty respect for the inviolable conscience of every individual.

3. *The necessity of education, including religious education, for all.* Once more the presence of this note within Protestantism from the earliest stages of its history can be amply documented. Luther's famous words in his "Address to the German Nobility" will do as well as any. He said: "I beg you all, my dear lords and friends, for God's sake to take care of the poor youth, and thereby to help us all. So much money is spent year after year for arms, roads, dams, and innumerable similar objects, why should not as much be spent for the education of the poor youth? . . . The word of God is now heard in Germany more than ever before. But if we do not show our gratitude for it, we run the risk of sinking back into a worse darkness."

This appeal, as modern in its relevance as the morning's newspaper, not only reveals the emphasis in question, but also shows clearly the basis for it. It harks back to fundamental Reformation principles. For if the Bible is to be consulted as the sufficient guide in all matters of religion and morals, people must be able to read the Bible. And that means education. Furthermore, if every person has direct access to the throne of grace, he is, on the one hand, worthy of education, and, on the other hand, greatly in need of an informed mind and cultivated spirit, in order that he may approach the Holy of Holies aright. Starting where it does, Protestantism cannot well come out at any other point than a stress upon widespread educational opportunity. The universal priesthood of believers demands universal education.

Also, this education cannot stop with the impartation of secular culture; it must include religious education as well. For in authentic Protestantism religion is closely linked with the common life. The line of demarcation between sacred and secular tends to fade away, just as the line of separation between priest and people tends to disappear. It is not strange, therefore, that Protestant New England in the colonial period projected an educational system for all children with a religious motive and a substantial religious content, which was to become the prototype of the American public schools. Parenthetically we may remark that our present educational system does justice to the major values precious to Protestants with one glaring exception—namely, it fails to include religion as an organic part of general education. To this we shall have to return at a later point.

4. *The supremacy of democracy as a political system, a philosophy of education, and a way of life.* Without denying for a moment the valued contribution to the development of democracy made by non-Protestant groups and cultures and their rightful place in our national life today, it is still, I believe, a matter of record that the principles of Protestantism provided a strong impetus in the direction of democracy. And again the reasons do not lie far afield.

The Book itself is one explanation. For when the Bible is exalted as the source of religious authority, other authorities begin to totter on their thrones. Time and again within recent centuries Bible-reading men and women stood out boldly against princes and bishops, and either did away with them entirely or else severely limited the scope of their powers. If time permitted, I think I could list a number of unfortunate by-products of Protestantism's stress upon the Bible, but the gains have been tremendous. Not the least among them has been a flowering of the democratic impulse, of which many millions in America, as well as in distant lands, are today the beneficiaries.

Another explanation is enfolded within the principle of the universal priesthood of believers. In the first instance this is, of course, a religious doctrine. But when it is translated into the terms of government, it becomes political democracy. Each citizen counts as much as any other. The common will of all is the source and warrant of whatever scheme of government is devised. And those who hold a brief tenure of authority do so with the consent of the governed and ultimately for their good. This same principle, when translated into pedagogical terms, becomes a democratic philosophy of education. Just as in church each person finds an open way between himself and God, so in school each student finds an open way between himself and the truth. Wise and mature teachers can help him in his pilgrimage and share with him their most precious insights, but they have no right to thrust their own conclusions upon him except with his own self-induced and freely given consent. When translated into terms of day-by-day living, this same principle becomes the rich interplay of democratic neighborliness, each respecting the other and all together advancing the common life. In every sector of life Protestantism, in so far as it is true to itself, moves out by an inner necessity in the direction of democracy. It cannot do otherwise.

Thus far we have gone back through the centuries to locate the basic principles which informed Protestantism at its origin and have characterized it during the intervening years, whence in turn we drew certain axioms proceeding naturally from these fundamental doctrines. It remains for us to develop the specific meanings of these axioms for the interrelationships of education and religion in America. There are five such implications which deserve our special attention.

1. *A firm adherence to the principle of the separation of church and state.* Lest we become entangled in confusion over the meaning of the phrase, "separation of church and state," we may as well indicate at the outset the connotation which we intend it to have. For this purpose we can do no better than to quote a succinct statement from the significant report of the American Council on Education's Committee on Religion and Education.[2] This Committee which comprised within its membership representatives of the three major religious groups in America, declared itself on this point as follows: "The core of meaning in the doctrine of separation of church and state we believe to be this: there shall be no ecclesiastical control of political functions; there shall be no political dictation in the ecclesiastical sphere except as public safety or public morals may require it." This does not mean, I take it, that the church has no obligations to the state. It does not mean that religion shall have nothing to say about the conduct of governmental affairs. Neither does it mean that the state must be indifferent to the interests of religion. It does signify that the church as an institution and the state as an institution must retain their respective autonomies in such a fashion that neither controls the other.

[2] Committee on Religion and Education, *The Relation of Religion to Public Education, the Basic Principles, Reports of Committees and Conferences,* American Council on Education Studies, Series I, IX, 26, Washington, D.C., 1947.

To this doctrine Protestantism, with scarcely a dissenting voice, gives its hearty approval. Indeed, being what it is, it could hardly countenance any other position. For this is the only *modus vivendi* as between church and state which promises to insure liberty of conscience for each individual, and respect for the conscience of every other. If a church—any church—gets control over the machinery of government, freedom of conscience goes out the window for all except the fortunate members of the dominant religious group. And if the state lords it over the church, freedom of conscience straightway evaporates for everyone except the fortunate few who rule the state. The sincere commitment of Protestantism to the separation of church and state stems directly from the cardinal values it cherishes.

By this I do not mean to suggest that Protestants alone subscribe to this doctrine. In his fair and comprehensive three-volume work entitled, *Church and State in the United States,*[3] Canon Stokes says: "In general it is noticeable that Jews in the United States generally take the position of Protestants on Church-State issues rather than that of Roman Catholics." However, this judgment is tempered by quotations like the following from Cardinal Gibbons: "American Catholics rejoice in our separation of Church and State, and I can conceive of no combination of circumstances likely to arise which should make a union desirable either to Church or State." Without imputing therefore to Protestants any monopoly on this belief, I can only say that they do hold it almost without exception, and that they must do so in order to be true to themselves.

But what does the separation of church and state mean within the field of education? What do Protestants take it to mean at the points most frequently discussed in the present hour?

I believe it can be said that an overwhelming preponderance of them, approaching virtual unanimity, hold it to signify that there should be no use of tax funds for the direct support or benefit of any sectarian school. The logic of their position is well expressed in a statement from James Madison's "Memorial and Remonstrance Against Religious Assessments," written in the summer of 1785.

---

[3] Canon Anson Phelps Stokes, *Church and State in the United States,* Harper & Brothers, 1950.

Mr. Madison said in part: "Who does not see . . . that the same authority which can force a citizen to contribute three pence only of his property for the support of any one establishment may force him to conform to any other establishment in all cases whatsoever?" In other words, the only way to guarantee ultimately the religious freedom of all American citizens is to decline to make any beginning in the direction of using funds contributed by all for the support of an educational institution maintained by any religious group.

As for the question of the propriety of using tax funds for the so-called auxiliary services, I cannot personally see any grave threat to our liberties in such a practice, provided the funds concerned are administered by the representatives of government and the services provided accrue to the benefit of persons as such, rather than of educational institutions and the churches which sponsor them. But I should hasten to add that this is a view which many Protestants do not share.

On the issue of weekday religious education, the majority opinion among Protestants would seem to be that no real violation of the separation of church and state is involved in such classes even when held on released time, provided that the opportunity for these classes is open to children and churches of all faiths on exactly the same terms, that no tax funds whatsoever are used for this purpose, and that the machinery of the public school system is not employed in any manner to promote or administer the classes in question. A very sizable minority within Protestantism would not concur in this position at all. But, speaking for myself, I can only record my conviction that if this were the most serious threat to religious liberty in American life today, we could account ourselves fortunate indeed.

2. *A strong devotion to a system of free public schools for all children.* This commitment arises naturally from several of the axioms previously listed as components of the point of view held by Protestants. We believe in education for all children and youth without exception. How best can this be provided? Through private schools run by an individual or a corporation from a desire for profit or else a motive of pure benevolence? Scarcely! If we depended

in any major degree upon institutions of this sort to meet our far-flung educational needs, the result would be pure chaos. Through parochial schools operated by a congregation or a communion to render service and promote its own special interests? Hardly! If we placed our chief reliance upon church institutions to educate the rising generation within a population of a hundred and fifty million people, the most likely result would be an almost equal degree of chaos. The only reasonable alternative, then, is the familiar array of public schools, supported by all the people and administered by the representatives of all the people.

We believe in democracy as a form of government. In what manner can a free people deal with the successive oncoming generations so as to fit them for the competent exercise of their citizenship and win their allegiance to the common good? The only procedure likely to accomplish these ends is a system of free schools, open to all, financed by all, conducted by officials in the name of all, and permeated by a high regard for the good of all.

We believe in toleration in the sense not of a patronizing condescension, but rather of a profound respect for differing opinions and beliefs. How best can a numerous people, spread over thousands of miles of mountains and prairie, and representing almost every race, nationality, and religious belief under heaven, insure such toleration? Only by seeing to it that our children and youth during their formative years rub shoulders with one another. America is often spoken of as the melting pot, and so it is. But there is one institution within American life to which the term is peculiarly suited —namely, our public schools. If it were not for the amalgamation accomplished there, the motto stamped on our coins and on our national existence as well, *e pluribus unum,* "out of many one," would probably become as dead as the Latin in which it is written.

By some such inner compulsions as these, Protestantism in the by and large has arrived at its sincere commitment to the American public school system. It is not, I believe, a superficial opinion, a thoughtless acceptance of the easiest way out, or an airy indifference to the importance of perpetuating the essential strains within the

Protestant heritage. On the contrary, it is rooted within that very heritage.

To be sure, quite a few upper class Protestant parents, along with those of other faiths, send their children at their own expense to private schools, paying meanwhile the taxes necessary to maintain the system they do not themselves patronize. In the same manner a small but growing number of Protestant communities, particularly those of the more markedly confessional groups, maintain parochial schools. But these exceptions are not sufficient to disprove the rule. The most conspicuous inconsistency between principle and practice in this regard would seem to be the hundreds of church-related colleges with which Protestantism has dotted the land. And yet even here the inconsistency may prove to be more apparent than real. After all, there is something to be said for the practice of taking a certain proportion of boys and girls at the age of eighteen, after they have spent twelve years in the democratic and democratizing experiences of public education during which their attitudes have been formed and their capacity for independent judgment developed, and immersing them in a somewhat sectarian atmosphere where they can learn more about their own distinctive heritage and fit themselves for effectual service to the church and the world.

The judgment, therefore, can apparently stand: both on principle and in practice Protestantism stands committed to our American public schools.

3. *A resolute conviction that these schools can and should include non-sectarian religious teaching as an organic part of their curriculum.* The best substantiation of this point is to be found in a series of quotations from the report of the Committee on Religion and Public Education of the International Council of Religious Education, submitted to this body at its 1949 meeting and approved by the representatives of thirty-nine Protestant communions in the United States and Canada and of thirty-two State Councils:

We believe that education is weakened and its usefulness impaired to the extent that it is separated from the disciplines and insights of religious faith.

We believe that religion is seriously weakened if it is not intimately related to general education.

Faith in God, the God of the Old and New Testaments, and faith in free men as His responsible creations have inspired our life and history from the early days of the nation and in its earlier Colonial history.

We expect that the schools will expose our children to this point of view. We go further in our expectations. As far as the school can, in view of the religious diversity of our people, judicial opinions, and our American traditions, we expect it to teach this common religious tradition as the only adequate basis for the life of the school and the personal lives of teachers, students, and citizens in a free and responsible democracy.

There is nothing in our laws, nothing in our court decisions up to and including the opinion of the United States Supreme Court in the Champaign case, nothing in our traditions, which prevents the school, within its own program, from making provision for the religious interpretation of life.

Several clear distinctions need to be made in regard to this semi-official declaration of Protestant policy. It calls for no sectarian teaching, not even anything distinctively Christian as opposed to Jewish. On the other hand, it presupposes an out and out theism and in other paragraphs expressly disavows any easy contentment with a vague "belief in spiritual values, conceived without reference to transcendent religious faith."

While it does not say so in as many words, it probably does not contemplate separate courses in the Bible or religious doctrine or any other religious subjects. Rather it points toward a positive handling of religious elements in our common heritage at whatever points they naturally belong to the on-going curriculum—religious classics and religious allusions in general classics within courses in literature; church and synagogue alongside all other community institutions in civics; the role of religious motivations on exactly the same basis as economic and political motivations in history; and the like.

Perhaps a word of special attention is due the claim that such a procedure is in full accord with American law and judicial decisions. The chief question on this point arises from Justice Black's majority opinion in the United States Supreme Court's decision on the Everson case, in which he interpreted the First Amendment to the Constitution as meaning that neither the Federal government nor a state government "can pass laws which aid one religion, aid all religions, or prefer one religion over another." [4] Of the three phrases, the middle one would block government from giving any aid to religion in general, and is the nub of the opinion for our present consideration. The point is that this ruling, in the judgment of able authorities, is open to serious question. Canon Stokes regards it as "a departure from established tradition," and thinks it likely to be overruled in the future. As a matter of fact, the Supreme Court itself in 1891 declared: ". . . no purpose of action against religion can be imputed to any legislation, state or national, because this is a religious people. This is historically true. From the discovery of this continent to the present hour, there is a single voice making this affirmation." [5]

Such a proposal, therefore, as the foregoing may with considerable assurance be regarded as fully legal, completely in accord with long established American tradition, desperately needed in the present crisis, and representative of the main body of Protestant sentiment. To express my personal views, as an officer of the International Council of Religious Education and as one who has given considerable thought to such a policy for some time, I find myself in hearty agreement with it. A number of Protestants, including some highly placed in both church and education, do not share this opinion. But a very great many do; and there is probably no proposal within the field of our present concern which so richly deserves the earnest exploration of Protestants, Catholics, and Jews alike as this one.

4. *A considerable reluctance to develop parochial schools.* Here, as elsewhere, Protestantism does not present a united front to the world. The best evidence suggests a rather rapid growth of such schools.

Nevertheless, the movement is still so small as to be almost negligible. And the prevailing trend of Protestant sentiment is in quite

[4] Everson v. Board of Education of the Township of Ewing et al., 330 U.S. 1, (1947) p. 15.
[5] Church of the Holy Trinity v. United States, 143 U.S. 457, (1891) p. 465.

the opposite direction. The same Committee of the International Council of Religious Education to which reference has already been made expressed itself forcefully on this subject: "Should our Protestant churches consider seriously the building of church-related elementary and secondary schools on an increasing scale? We believe our present answer should be 'No.' We defend the right of all religious groups to carry on church-related education at any level, elementary, secondary, or higher, and the right of parents to send their children to these schools if they so desire. But while we defend the right, we do not believe it should be widely exercised at the elementary and secondary levels." And—be it remembered—this report was approved by a very representative body of Protestant religious educators.

The logic of this position may be accurately described as simply the obverse of the Protestant commitment to public schools. Anything that stands to weaken this latter system is to be eyed with grave misgiving. And the widespread development of parochial schools would have precisely this effect. Each religious communion, as its own schools mushroomed, would probably become more and more restive under the double burden of taxation for public schools and voluntary support of parochial schools. The pressure upon politicians and legislators to employ tax funds for the financing of church schools would almost undoubtedly increase. And this would mark the end of American public schools as an effective instrument of the nation's life.

Furthermore, the end result would in all likelihood be a regrettable lowering of educational standards in general. We find ourselves even now in the grip of a serious educational crisis. We are hard put to it to discover enough good teachers for our public schools, as well as to pay them the salaries they deserve, and to provide the buildings and equipment required by our growing population. If this is the situation now, what would it be if we made any large scale effort to educate our children by religious groups? Except in small and homogeneous communities, such a policy would be expensive, inconvenient, and inefficient. Our present educational difficulties would increase. The educational level would decline. In short, elementary and secondary church schools constitute a minor and manageable problem only so long as they remain few in number. If the day should ever come when large segments of our population exercised their right to set up parochial schools, the only foreseeable outcome would be a major revolution in American public life. Other nations which are smaller, and more homogeneous in point of religious allegiance, and not accustomed to so many years of compulsory schooling may perhaps follow this line of development with a substantial measure of success. Apparently some have actually done so. But our situation is not theirs, and what has worked well for them will not assuredly do so for us. Indeed there is good reason to believe that it will not.

If a way is not found soon to reincorporate religion within the curriculum of general education, we may expect the Protestant sentiment in favor of parochial schools to grow. The rumblings of discontent with the current state of affairs are as yet low and indistinct. They may conceivably rise in volume and intensity. Therefore, it behooves religionists and educators alike to grapple with the major task of domiciling religion fully yet soundly within the public school system. Meanwhile Protestants generally shy away from the prospect of parochial schools on a large scale.

5. *A willingness to trust the church and the family for sectarian teaching.* We come finally to the allocation of ultimate responsibility for full-bodied religious instruction, and there are only two institutions which can accept this mandate—the church and the home. Many Protestants at this present juncture welcome weekday religious education, but they know full well it can supplement but never replace what is done elsewhere. Many also, as we have seen, earnestly long for the day when the literature, the history, the institutions, and the sanctions of religion shall be fairly and sympathetically dealt with in general education, so that our youth may receive their full birthright as they enter into their cultural inheritance. But they are well aware that such instruction can only, as someone has put it, lead pupils up to the door of church or synagogue; it cannot bid them enter. It can predispose them favorably toward the abiding worth of religion in personal and social life, and reduce somewhat the alarming spiritual illiteracy which now prevails, but

that is all. It cannot explicate and advocate specific doctrines, Methodist or Lutheran or Presbyterian, Protestant or Catholic, Christian or Jewish. And the reason is simple: we live in America. It cannot initiate children into the glorious mysteries of any particular liturgical forms. It cannot call upon the young to give themselves with wholehearted allegiance to any one church, creed, or savior.

And so we conclude with the only conclusion possible—the final, irreducible responsibility of church and home for religious nurture. Speaking for Protestants at least, I can say that both institutions have done many things which they ought not to have done, and left undone others which they should have done. At the present moment there is a vigorous new stress upon the family in Protestant circles. Almost every day it finds some new expression—a curriculum which requires the diligent cooperation of the families within a congregation; new materials and methods for counseling; novel devices for giving explicit help to families which are willing to make their home life religious. Nothing quite comparable is to be found at the moment within Protestant church-centered education, but rather a steady deepening of conviction and an unspectacular refinement of practice. We have far to go, but we are on the way.

Thus we come to the end of the course which we laid out before us. I can only voice the hope that, while not attempting to hide my personal opinions, I have achieved some measure of justice to the views of my fellow Protestants; and that I have done so in charity toward others who under different names and signs worship the same Lord; and that this venture in mutual understanding may set forward by a little the realization of the hopes and dreams which haunt us all alike.

VI

RELIGION IN A STATE UNIVERSITY

BY

J. HILLIS MILLER, PH.D.

President, University of Florida

During my graduate days at Columbia University, as I sat frequently at my window in a small apartment overlooking the vacant lot where the concrete foundations were being poured for the beautiful structure which is now the home of The Jewish Theological Seminary of America and The Institute for Religious and Social Studies, I had little thought that twenty-odd years later I would be writing a paper to be presented within the sacred walls of this great institution of higher learning. The historical fact of the matter is that I resented the whole procedure. The building, I reasoned, would soon obstruct the view from my window. Moreover, the blasting of stone and the sound of hammer were interfering with the business at hand. I am quite sure I saw no relationship between what I was doing at that time and the role I am playing today.

As a matter of fact, there *was* a relationship, and it may be said that I was at that time laying the philosophical basis for this paper. I was writing a book on "Radical Empiricism and Public Prayer." [1] My good friend and most admired personality, Harry Emerson Fosdick, the distinguished Chairman of the Executive Committee of The Institute for Religious and Social Studies, wrote a Preface to the volume and almost lifted it single-handedly to the position of "first choice" of the Religious Book of the Month Club. In that

[1] Later published under the title, *The Practice of Public Prayer,* Columbia University Press, New York, 1934.

book I tried to point out, in my immature way, that need, gratitude, devotion, and remorse are prevailing types of human experience which dominate the content of prayer in actual practice. None of these experiences is, as such, religious. They are universal in man's life, and hence naturally appear as the chief themes of prayer, commonly called "Petition," "Thankgiving," "Praise," and "Confession." Had I known then what I think I know now, with what erudition I would have pointed out that the neglect of religion in public education, and hence the failure to give these and other human reactions to our environment the religious sanctions they deserve, has led to rampant secularism in both education and life! Take, for example, gratitude and the modern temper. Twenty years ago, I wrote:

What Thanksgiving is, is simply illustrated by an incident in Robert Louis Stevenson's *Travels with a Donkey*. He had spent the night in the open wood. Feeling refreshed and exuberant in the morning when he awoke, he gave evidence of his appreciation by scattering some pennies around on the ground in payment for his lodging. The spontaneity of a natural gratitude was not destroyed by Stevenson's knowledge that no gratified deity would pick up the pennies.[2]

I went on to say:

This incident reflects the modern system of payment for services, and leads one to ask whether the expectation of payment for services rendered will undermine the custom of thanksgiving. Or to state the question a little differently, is thanksgiving genuine and spontaneous in a culture where mutual service and not generosity is customary? Is genuine gratitude expressed more adequately by prayers of thanksgiving than by "payment" or "service" for received goods? [3]

In the case of "Praise and the Glory of God," as a young author I was even more disrupting. I said:

Both the downfall of nationalistic theology and the rise of natural science have contributed to the tendency to shift from a God of natural power to a God of moral values, and consequently, the language of

[2] *Ibid.,* p. 98.
[3] *Ibid.*

praise becomes more humanistic and moralistic. The new cult of humanism growing out of liberal Protestantism and the Society of Ethical Culture growing out of liberal Judaism, together with a strong humanistic emphasis among all liberals, combine to make praise an appraisal of *man,* not of *nature.*[4]

To complete the story, I contended at that time that the value of confession in affording relief or forgiveness is a secondary consideration and raises an objective social problem:

The desire to exteriorize our sins or, to express it differently, to unburden the soul, is quite as genuine a human phenomenon as the feeling of guilt. The exteriorization process may continue even though forgiveness has been assured. Great sinners continue to recount their sins after their "conversion." Great sins furnish admirable subject matter for continued confession, and the great saints are conspicuous for their sinful youth. Sackcloth and ashes, prolonged fasting, and recurring visits to the confessional give evidence of the existence of more than a feeling of guilt. A classical illustration of this aspect of confession is, of course, the "Ancient Mariner." So determined was the Mariner to unburden his soul that he stopped everyone he met and compelled them to hear his penance. Prayer to heaven did not suffice, for he demanded pity and relief rather than forgiveness. The more he told his tale, the more obsessed with his crime he became.

> "I pass, like night, from land to land;
> I have strange power of speech;
> The moment that his face I see,
> I know the man that must hear me:
> To him my tale I teach." [5]

Please do not believe that a kind of nostalgia has taken possession of me and has alone prompted these references. I hasten to contend that they are offered also for the purpose of showing how easy it is for the secularized mind of man to invade even the sacred precinct of religion itself. If this be true of men and women who are professed adherents of religious faiths and religious institutions, how much easier it is for those who have escaped religious teachings and

[4] *Ibid.,* p. 135.
[5] *Ibid.,* pp. 157 f.

religious experiences altogether to adopt and live by secular philoso-
phies and humanistic beliefs.

We speak of secularism today as though it came in one package.
As a matter of fact, there are different kinds of secularism. It is probably more accurate to say that there are gradations of secularism
and that the various types are distinguishable. All the types seem to
feed upon man's humanistic tendencies. The first type, as we have
already pointed out, is closely identified with religion itself. Man's
reaction to his environment—that is, his expressions of need, gratitude, devotion, and remorse—may or may not receive religious sanctions. Even if they receive religious sanctions they may be slanted
in the direction of humanism. There is great significance in this
trend in and of itself. However, its greatest value to us in this discussion lies in the fact that so many men and women balance themselves precariously on the borderline between religion and moral
goodness.

There is a second level or second type of secularism. The good
person, that is, morally and ethically good, may ignore religion altogether. He does not give his human impulses a religious sanction, but
he is good nonetheless. This type of secularism denies the relevance
of religion to many areas of human activity. It assumes that religion will continue to evidence itself in fundamental beliefs, in
moods of reverence, and in specific religious observances. Politics,
business and industry, and other broad patterns of group behavior,
on the other hand, are no longer responsive to definite religious
sanctions. This is not to deny religion—it is to ignore it. This type
of secularism was admirably described by the editor of this series,
F. Ernest Johnson, in his introductory address, when he said:

> . . . there are educators of undoubted competence and devotion to
> their tasks who just have no interest in religion, period. Everything that
> goes by the name of religion leaves them cold. It is not a matter of being
> anti-religious, any more than tone-deafness is a matter of being anti-
> musical. They are not hostile to religion; they are simply bored by it. Just
> as a person may become absorbed in business, in scientific research, or
> in sports, to the exclusion of other cultural interests, so these educators
> regard religion as something entirely expendable. . . . Their attitude

is typical of contemporary secularism in the common meaning of that word, which I take to be indifference to religion as irrelevant to the main business of living.[6]

This form of secularism, the form that ignores religion, is not so dangerous from a philosophical point of view, but exceedingly dangerous from a practical point of view. It does not seek to destroy religious faith or religious institutions, but rather to isolate them from politics, business, and education. It seems clear that the practice of this philosophy would tend inevitably toward the eclipse of religion by ignoring it as an essential part of the culture and rendering it innocuous.

There is a third type of secularism which may be termed political or institutional. Secularism, in the sense of a political ethic or philosophy, has had an historical or evolutionary development of which the Supreme Court decisions represent the latest stage. This historical development is traced in consecutive steps by Agnes E. Meyer in an article in *The Atlantic Monthly*.[7] In this article she is inclined to contend that secularism was not invented by "Materialistic America." She seems to think that it began in the late Middle Ages in the philosophy of Duns Scotus, who taught that reason can operate in the realm of verifiable experience, quite apart from the sphere of faith posited on ecclesiastical authority. This may have been the beginning of the modern scientific spirit.

The second step, thinks Mrs. Meyer, took place when St. Thomas Aquinas proclaimed that the state has positive functions of perpetuating orderly social conditions in this world, and thereby, for the first time, challenged the authority of the church.

Another phase of the development may have taken place when Hugo Grotius declared that the law of nature was the product of reason and a principle of morality pursuant to which there developed the independent sovereign state.

John Locke and his followers furthered the development of the

---

[6] Cf. "Statement of the Problem," by F. Ernest Johnson, pp. 3–4.

[7] Agnes E. Meyer, "The School, The State, and The Church," *The Atlantic Monthly*, Boston, November, 1948, p. 49.

concept of the sovereign state to the extent that innumerable faiths could live peaceably together within the sovereign state. The influence of these European developments was felt in America through Jefferson and the other Founding Fathers. They made absolute the separation of church and state, reasons Mrs. Meyer, and the recent Supreme Court decisions have upheld the verdict.

Mrs. Meyer outlines this historical development to the satisfaction of many in the following paragraph:

> Our secular institutions are no mere accident but the finest product of five centuries of thoughtful statesmanship. They emerged out of the necessity to create harmony among diverse economic, philosophic, social and religious beliefs. Freedom in each one of these areas is possible only because the secular world creates an equilibrium of complementary forces. Its outstanding characteristic is its humane attitude of the happy mean. The secular ethic asks itself how conflict can be solved with the least damage to all concerned. The ethic of religious organizations asks itself who is right or wrong according to its various forms of absolutes! Since these absolutes are not subject to analysis, the churches create an *impasse* when they try to force their absolutes on our secular society. They become intransigent propagandists in a democratic world that can function successfully only when all clashing elements are willing and able to compromise.[8]

That is what is meant by secularism in the political sense, and, we might add, as viewed by a confirmed secularist. This type of secularism is supposed to be the protector of the freedom of the human spirit, as well as the protector of the freedom of divergent groups and faiths. To many, this autonomy of the state—its freedom from ecclesiastical control, and the freedoms for individuals and groups which it makes possible—represents the most precious values in the world. This may be true, but we are inclined to contend that the state's freedom from ecclesiastical control, and the freedom for individuals and groups which it makes possible, are values obtainable in other ways in a religious society. Many of us cannot yield to the secularists by saying that the churches cannot function democratically in a democratic world.

[8] *Ibid.*

Therefore, we are constrained to believe that the values outlined by Mrs. Meyer are bought at a very high price, if political secularism is the only way they can be bought. However, we believe that the development of public, secular schools and universities and the corresponding decrease in the influence of church-related schools have thrown this whole matter into a different focus. We believe that the elimination of the public schools and the state universities as avenues for the promulgation of the great religious heritage of our people, has led to the secularization of life that will result eventually in the wholesale destruction of a concern for moral, ethical, and spiritual values—that there will come a time when there will be nothing for the great sovereign, secular state to protect by means of all of its reasonable, logical, and protective theories and devices.[9]

Political secularism is related to the type of secularism practiced by the individual when he ignores religion. In its political form, secularism means that the state and all its institutions ignore religion and that they are presumably forced to do so by law. These agencies of the state, charged with the responsibility of transmitting the culture, are advised that there is a part of the culture, namely, that part that has to do with religion, that must be ignored. The social tragedy of this is that human products of such institutions will most likely go on through life ignoring religion because it is not a part of their knowledge, their intellectual experience, or their intelligent concern.

There is a fourth type of secularism that denies religion altogether. This brand of secularism denotes a philosophy of life which has no place for religious creeds or for religious institutions. It is a completely non-religious way of life. It carries its own ethical standards by which men may live quite apart from traditional religion. This type of secularism presupposes that men shall seek only human and natural ends. It assumes that all ends that transcend nature and human life are illusory. It is opposed to all belief in religious supernaturalism and philosophical idealism. The realities of the natural

[9] This summary was first developed by the author for an address at the University of Minnesota and published in *Religion in the State University*, edited by Henry E. Allen, Burgess Publishing Company, Minneapolis, 1950.

order, according to this form of secularism, have no relationship to an eternal and divine purpose. The uniqueness of the human spirit, affirmed by philosophical idealism, is also denied. Secularism, in this sense, is what is left over after these two religious and philosophical realities are abandoned.[10]

To put it another way, this type of secularism is based on the assumption that sense experience is our sole proof of truth, that material reality is the only reality, and that the only values are pragmatic enjoyments of a this-worldly type, which is immediately experienced and hedonistic in character. Secularism, in this sense, we believe, is also reinforced by a mistaken view of science. Because natural science studies phenomena which are verified through the senses and neglects other aspects of life, it is falsely assumed that no other aspects exist. Neglect, methodological omission, means denial of spiritual reality. This naturalistic philosophy may be taught in the public schools and the State universities with impunity, according to its advocates. If this were done, historical or institutional religion would be referred to, as is all too often the case, as an historical error which has been exposed at last by the extreme, though pious, secularists.

When the exclusion of religion and the inclusion of naturalism are combined to create the environment in which students are educated, we have the situation described so aptly by Doctor James A. Pike when Chaplain of Columbia University:

We are seeing the strange emergence of one religion—secularism—turned into a compulsory option in our academic scene. This, clearly, is no longer academic freedom. The Christian faith (and we would contend every other faith as well) has every right, even under the sanction of free inquiry into truth, to claim a hearing. Let secularism, or Mohammedanism, or Marxism, or what you will, remain an optional view of man and his world, taught as such in our free universities. Christians should welcome open confrontation between their faith and its rivals. A University is not a Sunday School. But the Christian faith should have a place among the live options placed before the student inquirer. Aca-

---

[10] See the inaugural address of George Finger Thomas, Professor of Religious Thought in the Harrington Spear Paine Foundation, *Religion in an Age of Secularism,* Princeton University, 1940, p. 9.

demic freedom should, by definition, imply at least this (parentheses mine).[11]

While I agree in principle, I would wish to expand his concept of academic freedom. My view on this subject created something of a ripple on the academic sea a year or so ago when I approached the subject of academic freedom from the point of view of the needs of students rather than from the point of view of the rights of the professor. I do not deny the right of a professor to teach objectively the truth wherever it may be found. However, this right is merely a corollary to the right of a student to acquire human knowledge from all possible sources. That students should also be given the basis for value judgments, is taken for granted, but that they should not be denied access to knowledge of any kind, is the heart and soul of any defense of academic freedom. To deny academic freedom to the teacher at the level of higher education, is to deny the student the full right to the expansion of mind and the complete basis for making value judgments of a discriminating kind. In these terms, academic freedom is not an end in itself, but a means to the greater end of preparing students to take responsibility for themselves and for the world which they have inherited from us.

The tendency to secularize basic human reactions, to ignore religion, to deny religion, and the tendency to secularize education by force of law, can lead to a moral depravity in the culture and to wickedness in the high and low places where men live and move and have their being. Moral depravity in our own nation resulted in organized racketeering in 1949 which totaled forty-five billion dollars, or twenty-five per cent of all expenditures by the American people. Regardless of what one's personal opinion might be of the Kefauver Senate Committee, it cannot be denied that widespread racketeering has been exposed and that public officials and law enforcement officers have been involved.

The conviction of two members of Congress for the use of official influence in obtaining money in connection with contracts and for government salary "kickbacks" has underlined our moral degeneracy

[11] From his opening sermon, October 2, 1949, quoted by Canon Theodore Otto Wedel, *The Place of Religion in a University*, p. 6.

in high places. While one of these convicts was still in prison, he was lauded by a fellow Congressman as a great and loyal American. A major general of the United States Army Air Force has been convicted of illegally and immorally using his position to make personal profits during wartime. We have Alger Hiss, Judy Coplon, and the others who have sold their country for a few pieces of silver. We have those, like the grocer in Cleveland, who boosted the price of bread to a dollar a loaf and milk to a dollar a quart in the time of a great storm when his fellow Americans were hungry and cold. We have political elections won by those who would buy their way into office or degrade their opponents with obvious lies and unbelievable distortions. We have many Americans, among them philosophers and scientists, who are leading other Americans away from God and toward spiritual weakness and moral degeneracy and ruin. The tragedy of it all is that there are too many Americans who are inclined to pass lightly over the decline in morals among our people, which may spell disaster for this nation if we do not come to our senses and change the trend. Arnold J. Toynbee, historian and philosopher, has said, that every one of the twenty-one civilizations he has studied failed because of its decline in moral and spiritual judgments.

It was not my intention to dwell at such length upon the state of our society when I began this discussion. One is, however, carried forward by a kind of moral compulsion to explore for himself the conditions against which the forces of education must somehow be arrayed, if we are to reverse the trend of secularism and moral disintegration which have beset us. May we now explore the role of the state university in this process?

The untrammelled acquisition and dissemination of truth has long since been the major role of the university. The question now arises as to the lines along which truth is to be most vigorously pursued. Are we to continue the pursuit, as we have so exclusively done in the past, of the nature of the physical universe? Or must we marshal more of our forces in pursuit of a knowledge of the nature of man and the values he must respect? And does the state of our nation and our world have anything to do with our emphasis? If we are compelled to direct more attention toward man and his values, how can we have a clear, positive moral and spiritual affirmation in academic life? Some way must be found to combine the intellectual and moral correlatives for the disinterested pursuit of truth. Edmund E. Day, wise and seasoned educational statesman, has shown us the way in a recent address. On this occasion Dr. Day said:

There are intellectual and moral correlatives to the disinterested pursuit of truth which have not yet been sufficiently recognized. The truth-seeker is expected to exhibit an open mind, highly receptive to evidence, a habitual suspension of judgment until dependable evidence is in hand, a tolerance for honest differences of opinion, a stout resistance to bigotry or fanaticism. His should be a mind capable of sustained calm, critical, reflective and imaginative thinking. These are intellectual imperatives for the scholar and scientist in his own field; they should characterize the intellectual activities of scholars and scientists outside their specialties. What is more, every effort should be made to induce these same qualities of mind in all the learners who come to our colleges and universities. There is a profound mental disturbance in contemporary society. People are troubled, confused, distrustful. More and more they are showing symptoms of hysteria, if not of paranoia. Now if ever is the time for keeping our individual and collective heads clear and straight. . . .

The *moral* correlatives of complete devotion to the truth seem to me equally clear. How can a person be a genuine truth-seeker who is not in all connections completely honest and honorable? How can a true scholar, scientist or teacher be wanting in personal integrity? These same traits of character and others basically related to human relationships in a democracy, should be an essential part of the product of general education at all levels. Ways and means of obtaining them by formal education in and out of the classroom demand more attention than they have had. For freedom imposes its moral as well as its intellectual imperatives, and the liberty we have treasured is not likely to be retained without an individual and social discipline of mind and spirit to which education must contribute with all the power it can possibly muster.

In the kind of world we now face higher education cannot afford to be neutral with respect to the intellectual, moral and spiritual issues of our time. It must do more than demand freedom. It must act positively in terms of the responsibilities freedom imposes. It must assert a constructive leadership of its own in thwarting the attack the Communists are making on the whole intellectual, moral and spiritual structure of society.[12]

If this is the new role of higher education in this troubled world, and I confidently believe it is, it is our job as educators to proceed to discharge it. Moreover, I see no way for us to discharge this responsibility if we try to dilute religion, ignore it, deny it, or to set up barriers against its consideration as a basis for the moral and spiritual imperatives referred to by Dr. Day in the statement quoted above. This issue must be faced head on.

What are the prohibitions against the inclusion of religion in the State university? It is my conviction that none of the types of secularism described in this chapter are insurmountable if we can solve the political problem of the true significance of the separation of church and state. There is a serious conviction in my mind that the separation of public education from ecclesiastical control is not synonymous with the separation of religion from education. In holding this conviction, I am also convinced that one can contend that the heterogeneity of our religious heritage has established the political separation of church and state beyond debate. It is our duty as educators to understand and to define this policy. I give you my own interpretation:

Virginia has been given credit for achieving the equality of the religious sects. This concept was written into the Statute of Religious Freedom in 1786. The Philadelphia Convention in 1787 wrote these experiences in Virginia into the Constitution of the United States. To make absolutely sure that religious liberty was secure, the First Amendment to the Constitution was ratified in 1791. This action still left the States each free to maintain a religious establishment until they decided to abolish it themselves through the instrument of the Fourteenth Amendment.

After all these things had been done, it is interesting to observe

[12] Edmund E. Day, "The Long-Range Role of Higher Education," *Higher Education in the National Service,* Report of a National Conference of University and College Administrators and Educators, Government and Military Officials, and representatives of national organizations, American Council of Education Studies, Series I, 44, Washington, D.C., 1950, pp. 47 f.

what happened in the State of Virginia and particularly at the University of Virginia. In doing so let us bear in mind the fact that the University was founded by Thomas Jefferson and that Jefferson wrote much of the legislation referred to above. Jefferson was Chairman of the Board of Visitors of the University, and in that capacity he wrote the report of the Board and said that the Professor of Ethics at the University was to teach "the proof of the being of God, the creator, preserver, and supreme ruler of the universe, the author of all the relations of morality, and of the laws and obligations these infer." Moreover, he established a practice which has been followed to this day, when he invited the various religious sects in the State to establish, near the university, schools for "further instruction in their own particular tenets."

We have been terribly confused about this matter, and the confusion has been due largely to the fact that politicians and zealous churchmen have been rather determined to use the words, "church," and "religion," as synonyms. The church is the organized institutional expression of religion, and to say that the state must be free of control by this institution, and the church of control by the state, is not the same thing as contending that the state must be free from and have no part in religion. It is my belief that Justice Hugo Black fell into this error in the McCollum case and used the terms, "church," and "religion," interchangeably.

Therefore, we believe that our forefathers' concern for the equality of religious sects should not be construed as the "separation of church and state." It was considered in those early days, and should be so construed now, as the guarantee for the political equality of all religious groups. I do not believe there was ever any intention that religion was to be excluded from public education. We like the way Charles H. Wesley summarized the situation when he said: "As a result of this history, we now know that this doctrine of separation does not mean that the State is opposed to or indifferent to religion, and we also know it does not mean that Church and State are to exist in watertight compartments." [13]

[13] Charles H. Wesley, "Religion and Education," *Christian Education,* Philadelphia, September, 1948, p. 182.

YORK COLLEGE LIBRARY

While it is true that the most troublesome problem is that growing out of the political issue of church and state, there are three phases of this problem that make it difficult for the State university to deal effectively with religion. It is true that these secondary problems would not loom so large if the major problem were solved; nevertheless, they are problems that would have to be reckoned with under any circumstances if effective work is to be done in the university.

The first of these secondary considerations is the same old difficulty of giving students the necessary preparation in high school for work at the college level. This has been a major problem in English, and other languages, in mathematics and the basic sciences, and in many other fields in which effective work in college is conditioned upon effective work being done at the secondary level. But this raises the major issue in this series of lectures and is being discussed by competent authorities. I mention it here because it has a bearing on the whole subject of religion at the college level. Many are inclined to think that religion can be taught in the colleges and universities with less difficulty than it can be taught in the elementary and secondary schools. Theoretically this is true, but in reality few sequential subjects can be taught effectively in college, if they are not first of all adequately taught in the public and private schools at the lower level. This is true of religion.

Another secondary problem—secondary in the sense that there is little need for solving it until we have established the freedom to teach religion at all levels—is the problem of training staff members capable of teaching religion. Just as important as the ability to teach religion is the ability to deal with religion in connection with other subjects such as history, philosophy, literature, and sociology. Even if we are free to teach religion, we must have capable teachers. This means, we venture, that our teacher-training institutions and our college teacher-training processes must first of all be organized to deal effectively with religion. Here, again, it is hoped that others lecturing in this series will point the way. This phase of the total problem has a definite bearing upon the university problem of how to deal effectively with religion.

The third difficulty, which may or may not be considered secondary, is the whole problem arising out of any discussion of the new role of higher education in these times. There must be some way to orient the entire university to the need for dealing with the moral, ethical, and spiritual values of man. We have in mind the institutional point of view, which is essential even when we have the right to teach religion as the basis for moral, ethical, and spiritual values. It is essential even when we have religion adequately taught in the public and private elementary and secondary schools. It is essential even when we have solved the problem of teacher training. It is just as essential to have the religious point of view as a part of institutional policy, if religion is to be sympathetically considered, as it is to have the personnel point of view as a part of institutional policy, if a strong personnel program is to be developed on the campus as a part of the total educational process.

Psychologically what we are contending is clear. It is not enough to have the right or the freedom to act. There must be the will to act and, what is just as important, the ability to act. This is true with respect to any aspect of higher education. Religion is no exception. An understanding of the need for religion, the freedom to deal with it effectively, and the desire and ability to deal with it, are all part and parcel of the procedure we must follow, if we are to see to it that the graduates of our State universities combat secularism in our society by means of the moral, ethical, and spiritual prejudices in their lives and their works.

I have made some explicit statements concerning the place of religion in a State university, and I have outlined the responsibility of the university as regards moral and spiritual values in our troubled world. The reader would be justified in asking me to state how we deal with religion in our own institution. I have a statement which I use from time to time to outline our procedure. You have a right to hear it.

The University of Florida does not claim any superiority over other institutions in dealing with religion. It has developed a program over the years that seeks to give religion its rightful place in the total program of the University. Whether or not this claim is justified must necessarily be left to others, who can view our program more objectively. We do sense a responsibility at this time to describe it briefly. For fifteen years the University has had in its University College a program of general education with its core curriculum and its responsibility for providing necessary foundational preparation for our many upper division schools and colleges.

We confess a conservative approach. As Dean Winston W. Little of the University College contends, we still look to our traditional heritage as the source of our values. He likes to refer to Lewis Mumford's definition of a liberal in education, namely, he who seeks new arrangements only that the spirit of old values may live. "Regarding ends to be sought," Dean Little writes, "general education attempts to develop a socially sensitive layman, to contribute to that part of one's education that looks to his life as a responsible human being and citizen."

In the sophomore year this program of general education, which includes comprehensive courses in American institutions, physical sciences, practical logic, biological sciences, to mention only some of them, offers a comprehensive course called "The Humanities." This course is divided into two parts. One semester is concerned with "Our Cultural Heritage," and a second semester is given over to a consideration of "The Humanities and Contemporary Life." The first semester is further divided into units concerned, respectively, with (a) The Greek View of Life, (b) The Medieval and Renaissance Views of Life, and (c) Rationalism and the Romantic View of Life. The second semester is divided into the following units: (a) The Conflict of Reason and Appetite or Will in Contemporary Life, (b) The Conflict of Individual Interest and Group Welfare in Contemporary Life, and (c) The Contemporary Interpretation of the Dignity of Man and the Worth of Life. It will be seen that we seek in this course to review the system of values of those who helped to create our cultural heritage and that we deal realistically with the conflict of values in contemporary life.

In the absence of time to discuss this matter further, we are constrained to assert rather dogmatically that in our judgment this program provides an almost ideal opportunity to give religion its proper place in an analysis of our cultural heritage and our contemporary scene.

The second consideration given to religion on the campus of the University of Florida is in the Department of Religion in the College of Arts and Sciences. The teaching of courses in religion at this level is a further attempt to acquaint the student with the traditional religious cultures of the past, so that he will be aware of the part which religion has played in the development of civilization in various parts of the world. From this historical background, it is then possible to examine the problems of religion in relation to contemporary living. It is hoped that from studies of this type students may be broadly oriented for life and work, faith, and discipline.

The Department of Religion now offers eight courses, all of which are entirely elective. Two courses entitled, "The Religious Foundations of Modern Life," are introductory to the field, and they cover religious history and thought from early Judaism to modern times. Three courses in the Bible are offered: "The Old Testament in the Light of Today," "The Career and Significance of Jesus," and "Christianity and the Greco-Roman World." Two courses in comparative religion are available, the first of which presents a survey of the major religions of the world, and the second of which offers students an opportunity to explore specific religious principles which give uniqueness to the important cultures of the world today. The final course, entitled "Problems of Religious Philosophy," is designed to explore the important contemporary philosophical and theological issues in American religious life.

It is possible for a student to major in religion in the College of Arts and Sciences, but there are only a few cases in which this seems justified. A number of students elect religion as one of three subject fields in which to take a group major. Pre-theological students are usually limited to a maximum of four courses in religion, in order that they may gain a broader training in related fields while undergraduates. No graduate work, *per se,* is offered in religion, although a number of students elect it as a minor when graduate degrees are obtained in such fields as education, sociology, and psychology. Students who take two or three courses in the Department as electives come from the various colleges in the University.

The third aspect of the program of religion on the campus of the University is represented by The Student Religious Association. This organization has an Executive Committee of fifteen members representing the various religious groups on the campus. It is this organization that promotes all-University programs, arranges for speakers, and organizes discussion groups in the fraternity houses, dormitories, and other living quarters. It also arranges for a Religious Emphasis Week once during the college year with a battery of outstanding religious leaders. It was this group that encouraged the appointment on the University staff for a semester of Dr. T. Z. Koo, one of the great religious spirits of this generation.

The University of Florida has won national recognition for its student government organization and activities and for its student Honor System. In this organization the students themselves have not ignored religion. On the President's cabinet you will find a Secretary of Religious Affairs. Through this student government official there is a very close relationship between Student Government and the Student Religious Association.

It is extremely important that the administration of a State university exhibit a vital concern for religion, and that staff members be selected on the basis of *what they are* as well as on the basis of *what they know*. At the University of Florida we do not care *what* religious faith staff members hold, but we are concerned that they have some sense of the importance of religion in personal and social life.

The University of Florida has encouraged another development. Instead of urging the leading denominations to erect great churches at the entrance to the campus, it has encouraged them to erect lovely, practical, and useful student centers in close proximity to the campus. Six denominations have already acted in accordance with this policy. These houses furnish opportunity for religious activities which supplement denominational worship in the churches of the city. They meet a real need and they have contributed without doubt to the spirit and atmosphere of the campus itself.

I have reason to believe that the emphasis on religion at the University of Florida is playing a part in the lives of students. Let me conclude with one bit of evidence. Last year [1950] the students invited me to speak at a religious service in the auditorium of Florida Union at midnight on the night before the University adjourned for the Christmas holidays. I accepted, and when I appeared I was greeted by an audience that filled the auditorium and overflowed into the halls. It was not a large auditorium, but the experience was impressive. This year I was invited to speak again at midnight— this time in the University Auditorium. Approximately one thousand students and faculty members were assembled, and in appropriate silence they listened as I attempted to discuss the importance of religion in the lives and thought of those who are soon to go forth to help shape the destiny of our world.

We know pretty well by this time in the history of our nation what secularism is like and what it is doing to our people. We have spent an endless amount of time discussing the reasons for its prevalence. We believe that the most important corrective lies in the educational process. We believe that there are few prohibitions against the inclusion of religion in the educational process, particularly at the college level. And we believe that it is the role of education in these times to do something about this problem. The alternative to doing something about it is not pleasant to contemplate. There may be nothing less at stake than the future of our civilization.

VII

RELIGION IN MUNICIPAL COLLEGES

BY

ORDWAY TEAD, LL.D.

Chairman, Board of Higher Education, City of New York

I wish it were possible for us physically to conduct this occasion in one of the four city colleges. I allude here to the College of the City of New York, Hunter College, Brooklyn College, and Queens College. Only so could I convey to you vividly the peculiar quality of life and sentiment which we in the city colleges confront. It is vital to realize that our students come to us each day from widely diverse homes and neighborhoods.

They come from a representative cross-section of local backgrounds; they are of different races, religions, colors; they have had different educational and cultural experiences; and they represent different economic levels and interests. This means, as related to our theme, that our student bodies comprise those interested in, neutral or indifferent to, as well as those aggressively opposed to religion in its organized and traditional expressions. Theistic, humanistic, agnostic, atheistic—all outlooks are represented; and all those young people are studying in peace and goodwill together. Our campuses are a living demonstration that what unites us all in the cause of higher education is a bond which, at least on the campus, takes precedence over, cuts across, and in some way transcends whatever may be the divisive factors of doctrine or belief.

It was a sound impulse which guided President Shuster of Hunter College to have engraved in stone on the outside of the Park Avenue building the sentence by Ralph Waldo Emerson, "We are of different opinions at different hours, but we may always be said to be on the side of truth." Indeed, if religion is deemed to have something to do with truth-seeking, our colleges are related in some fundamental and organic way to the religious enterprise, when that is deeply conceived. One emphasis I propose to stress is that education can never cease to be at bottom a moral effort; and however much it may seem to be secularized, it nevertheless partakes at its best of a process and quality of commitment, of devotion, of responsibility, of purposefulness, yes, and of affirmative dedication, which come close to the essence of something which may truly be called a religious outlook.

The fact that all involved—teachers and students—may not at all times realize the full implication of their attitudes and labors in these directions, does not alter the reality that a college is justified as an institution supported by society only as it demonstrates from time to time and in protean ways that its purpose is to give light and guidance to the minds and hearts of those who are struggling in the human situation. Moreover, if there is a crisis in the college world today—as I agree there is, as Sir Walter Moberly states in the title of his well known book, *The Crisis in the University* [1]—it arises because there have been fumbling, confusion, and forgetfulness on the part of too many of the participants as to why the college exists and what they are supposed to do about it.

The crisis, we may almost say, is not one of excessive secularization, though that is a fact. It is one of failure to keep crystal clear the basic purpose of higher education. And that purpose—irrespective of one's theology or faith—is the cultivation of rational and deeply felt drives, commitments, and zeal, toward realizing the good life on earth.

If we are concerned with reverent attitudes toward the cosmos and intelligently loving relations with our fellow men universally regarded, the problem of religion in public colleges is one that is wide open for constructive consideration. If, on the other hand, we are interested in the preservation and extension of those attitudes

[1] Sir Walter Moberly, *The Crisis in the University,* The Macmillan Company, New York, 1949.

and actions which are dictated by sectarian, denominational, and institutional religious expressions conventionally viewed, the problem is of a different order; and I confess at once that from my own point of view it is in these latter terms completely insoluble.

I shall divide my presentation into two parts. The first will be a brief description of the institutional expression of religion in our city colleges. The second part will consist of some observations about the place and influence of what I shall call a high religious attitude in public colleges, on the part of students and faculty. In this second part, I shall consider (1) the qualities which we would like to see people develop in order to lead a good life; (2) what religion has to do with the development of those qualities; (3) what education tries to do about this same problem; (4) how we can further advance the effectiveness of education in the direction of the purposes suggested.

I

If I may be briefly statistical, our daytime liberal arts undergraduate bodies comprise a little over 30,000 students. And if to these are added those earning degrees in the evening and those taking adult education, non-credit courses, the number totals around 72,000 students. I shall center attention here on the daytime undergraduate situation, while recognizing that there is a certain amount of formalized religious activity carried on by and for evening students.

In each of the colleges, there are organized groups of Catholics under the designation of Newman Clubs, of Jewish groups in Hillel organizations, and of Protestant groups in both Christian Association activities and, to a lesser extent, in denominational clubs. The grand total of enrollment in these several organizations is somewhat under 4,000, but in recognizing how relatively small this figure is, it must always be remembered that many students with neighborhood parish ties may never seek the opportunity to affiliate themselves with the college religious organizations.

The physical facilities for conducting services, conferences, and club meetings for these religious groups are less adequate than we could wish. We have no student union buildings on our campuses. But in close geographical relation with each of the colleges, there are privately owned dwellings which have been put at the disposal of the colleges under what we term our "house plan" arrangement. The most commodious of these is the Roosevelt House of Hunter College, which functions deliberately as an interfaith meeting place.

Typically, each of these religious groups is aided by a faculty adviser who is a member of the same faith, and often by designated chaplains or religious directors, designated by the outside agency.

The time factor as to extracurricular gatherings of all kinds is one of the most hampering features, as usually the noon period on one day a week, from twelve to two o'clock, is all the time that is made available for such meetings. This is due, of course, to the fact that students scatter to their homes as soon as classes are concluded in the afternoon. We have no dormitory life except for one small unit for veterans at City College. This means, of course, that there is considerable competition among all sorts of clubs for the time of the students in this weekly noon period. Two of the colleges provide explicitly an active Interfaith Council, which seeks through occasional meetings to discover areas of common action and actually to conduct interfaith gatherings of various sorts.

On the score of formal instruction in the curriculum, there has until recently been little recognition of the religious element in life. But, increasingly, attention has been given to the literary aspects of the Bible in English courses. Brooklyn College has a course in comparative religion. And there is naturally some consideration of kindred problems in courses in philosophy, although, even here, a strongly humanistic and "scientific" approach is usually manifest.

When I have said all this, I have essentially summarized what goes on in our colleges directly identifiable as traditional religious activity. The great historic faiths, in other words, are recognized in our colleges, and to some extent those who affiliate themselves with these clubs come to have an intensified awareness of their religious tradition and distinguishing doctrinal beliefs.

Yet I personally cannot refrain from wondering whether this very intensification of awareness of the tradition of the respective religions may not give rise to influences which are to some extent unfortunate. It seems to me there is always the danger of fostering a certain separatism of outlook, a sense of exclusiveness, a sense of absolute and unique rightness. This may result from the feeling each group has, to put it bluntly—even though it is not expressed in these words— that it "thanks God we are not as other men are." I raise this question, because it seems to me that in colleges like these, there have inevitably to be confronted such questions as the following: Have those beyond the pale of the great religious faiths no open avenues to God, to committed devotion, to holiness and dedication? What happens spiritually and morally to those many young people who come from homes in which there is no church affiliation? Are they all "lost souls"? And is the college not responsible for sensitizing them to the great religious traditions and insights of human history?

I remind you again that our student body represents the indifferent, the atheist, the materialist, the Marxist, the logical positivist, the scientific humanist, the ethical culturist. Is some *theological* conviction to be made the key to identifying genuine religious vitality as we confront this varied assortment of approaches to life? My own answer, of course, is, "No."

Dr. F. Ernest Johnson in an earlier paper said this: "I am now ready to offer my principal proposition, that the divorcement between religion and education is the most basic defect in American life, the correction of which may reasonably be expected to do more than anything else to overcome the sickness of a secularist society." [2]

But I do think that this problem of divorcement needs careful analysis. Is the solution that each religious group should seek to maximize its own effort on the campus? Dr. Johnson made clear in the same paper that he did not mean that. Yet, in conventional terms, in the bringing together of religion and education, it would seem that those of the several historic faiths are basically trying to make better Jews, better Catholics, better Protestants. That is good

[2] "Religion and the Philosophy of Education," in *Science, Philosophy and Religion,* Conference on Science, Philosophy and Religion in Their Relation to the Democratic Way of Life, New York, 1940, pp. 336 ff.

and wholesome. But is that the only possible educational approach to the spiritual realities of our hearts and of our times?

II

After this descriptive statement, I proceed to the second part of the discussion and ask: What do we want people to be like, possessed of what splendid qualities, as they mature? Clearly, we want people to be responsible, ethically and morally, in the ordinary affairs of life —in their family living, at their work, as citizens, and in every other phase.

Such informed responsibility is essential; but we want also more friendliness and fraternal human relations which cut across every type of boundary. We want, in the sense that Albert Schweitzer has used the phrase, people who have "reverence for life." Surely we would also like to feel that more people have some deeply felt conviction of the meaning, direction, and significance of their own lives, and that they were committed to acting in the direction of the goals which they have established—committed, moreover, to the exercise of a thoughtful "know-how" to direct their action intelligently toward the fulfilment of life's meaning and of the goals they come to cherish.

The moral obligation to be intelligent is one of the claims that college people have to acknowledge, it seems to me, if they are to be the kind of people we want in our kind of society. That means, of course, that they will be mindful of the dignity and the integrity of every person. They have to be intelligently democratic in conducting their human relations, and scientific in their approach to mastery of their problems in the worlds of nature and human nature. All these qualities are not only admirable but essential to social living; and they have, therefore, to be held in mind as educational aims as we move on to certain other questions.

One of these necessary questions in relation to our theme is: What is religion concerned about? And what functional or developmental area does it occupy for all people in such a society as ours? In answer, I shall borrow from Alfred North Whitehead's *Re-*

ligion in the Making,[3] and suggest that for experience to have a religious quality, it has to be characterized by one or another or all of the following attributes: it has to do with our experience of aloneness; it has to do with our desire for something which calls forth community loyalty—the "wider loyalty" that we often stress; it has to do with a longing for some meaning in life; it has to do with the assurance that even in a world community each individual is himself uniquely valued. Those are the elements, says Whitehead, of the quality of living which is religious.

A further way of answering this question is helpfully supplied in a volume, *Religious Values in Education.*[4] Although the author employs a different vocabulary, his meaning comes close to agreement with Whitehead's position. He characterizes action which is religious as being that "creative social action" having to do with the effort to *value,* to *experience community,* to be *executive (i.e.,* effective in operation), to be *esthetic,* and to be *contemplative.* Clearly, if all productive experience that is characterized by one or another of these "modes" may be correctly identified as religious, the area of religious concern and responsibility is widened to be coterminous with life itself.[5]

It is in this same sense that President J. Seelye Bixler of Colby

[3] Alfred North Whitehead, *Religion in the Making,* The Macmillan Company, New York, 1926.

[4] Ward Madden, *Religious Values in Education,* Harper & Brothers, New York, 1951.

[5] A valuable and representative survey of the present diversity of religious views is to be found in "Religion and the Intellectuals," *Partisan Review Series No. 3,* New York, 1950, p. 138. In the final paper of this volume, Professor Paul J. Tillich concludes his statement with the following significant words:

Others are waiting for a religious answer which does not destroy reason but points to the depth of reason; which does not teach the supernatural, but points to the mystery in the ground of the natural, which denies that God is a being and speaks of Him as the ground and depth of being and meaning, which knows about the significance of symbols in myth and cult, but resists the distortion of symbols into statements of knowledge which necessarily conflict with scientific knowledge. A theology which takes this position, which preserves the intellectual honesty of the intellectual and expresses, at the same time, the answers to the questions implied in man's existence and existence generally—such a theology is acceptable to the intelligentsia (and to many non-intellectuals as well). It prevents the turn of the intellectuals toward religion from becoming a matter of romantic concessions or of self-surrender to authority.

College says, "Religion is devoted and loyal commitment to the best that reason and insight can discover."

If I have now offered some suggestion of a meaningful view of what religious experience is, it is next in order to inquire: What is the uniquely educational aspect of human experience? How does the task of education relate itself to the growth of religious expression in the sense above defined?

Professor Robert E. Mason, in *Moral Values in Secular Education* [6] says of higher education: "The supreme loyalty is to the free, critical human intelligence," and he goes on, "loyalty to, and faith in, criticism, experiment, public inspection (meaning public evaluation of ideals), group deliberation, will be the highest loyalty and deepest faith of educated youngsters" (parentheses mine). To which, my personal response is, God forbid! But I quote this as being a representative utterance reflecting the view of many committed to the purely intellectualistic approach to higher education. I propose that an adequate answer to the questions before us requires a broader statement.

There are, on the other hand, those expressions of the aims of higher education which come from the traditional religious sources, but which I have not time here to elaborate.[7] They do, however, all in varying ways relate the task of higher education to fulfilling and commending the message of the Christian faith, variously interpreted, to the mind and heart of the student.

Another, more qualified, yet spiritual, approach to the purposes of the college is expressed in the following paragraph from the Spring, 1950, Baccalaureate Sermon of President James B. Conant at Harvard. He there expresses his conviction that "a feeling that the universe is somehow so constructed that each and every act of a human being has cosmic significance, seems to me the minimum

---

[6] Robert E. Mason, *Moral Values in Secular Education,* Columbia University Press, New York, 1950, p. 133.

[7] See for one of the most vigorous of such statements, Howard Lowry, *The Mind's Adventure,* The Westminster Press, Philadelphia, 1950. See also, as representative, the address of Monsignor Fulton J. Sheen before the Eighty-Fourth Convocation of the Board of Regents of the State University of New York, "Education as the Guardian of the American Heritage," October 20, 1950.

basis on which the Christian tradition firmly rests. If you couple this with wonder at the unexpected glimpses of man's ability and desire to move at least occasionally towards unselfish ideals of conduct, you may then have faith that the sum total of the human drama seen over a sufficient span is not 'a tale told by an idiot full of sound and fury,' but on the contrary, has a purpose, though it be hidden from us."

Again, the more profound purposes and content of higher education can in considerable measure be expressed in terms of the acceptance and utilization of the whole spiritual contribution of Western civilization historically viewed. In the final chapters of Crane Brinton's *Ideas and Men*,[8] for example, will be found a summary of the deeper human meaning of this historical growth, which says much that is illuminating about the aims of higher education.

I shall, however, have to add a still further expression of what higher education is about, in order to relate its task as closely as I believe is necessary and desirable to the functional role of high religion in our society.

I start with the problem of the clarification and extension of values, and declare that man is a value affirming, a value cherishing, and a value realizing animal. He finds, therefore, value judgments to be essential, which means also that moral judgments based on some more or less adequate knowledge are integral to his living. The conscious identification of values thus becomes an imperative assignment, initially; and some basis for weighing and choosing among values is required ultimately. Also, the processes by which values are striven for through conscious effort cannot be ignored, nor can we fail to realize that for these values to have directive influence over conduct, they must have an appeal and an outcome which are clearly found to be desirable and satisfying to the individuals involved. Within education itself, moreover, there is the instrumental value of the aim of making people able to fulfil their several functional roles in society. Each individual is typically a worker, a citizen, a family member, a leisure-time person, and in his aloneness, he is a human soul.

[8] Crane Brinton, *Ideas and Men,* Prentice-Hall, New York, 1950.

These functional roles supply the clues and set the stage for the improvement of the competence of each of us, that development of each of us which *education* must largely provide. Some older educators resist and resent the notion that it is the task of higher education to interpret and make more effective the ability of people to live in these functional roles. Yet the more so-called "progressive" of the educators tend to think that this states the entire scope of wise objectives.

Moreover, in relation to the content of education, we have in historic experience built into the ideal meanings of certain concepts a nucleus of values which as a society we strive continuously to make influential. In our American society, some of the most important of these concepts, symbolized and summarized in words, have come to identify widely shared values. I refer to such words as democracy, freedom, love, science, rationality, leadership, personality, community, creative art, cultural pluralism, and world organization.

The mere mention of these concepts suggests that if they are to be realized, they have to be *understood* in their operating, know-how phases. The grasping of the "executive" or operative ways and means of better living thus becomes one crucial assignment of higher education. And if such values as these are to be controlling, individuals have to be literally *possessed by them,* so that they will be effective in action and satisfying in outcome.

If values are to be known as good, and if they are to be truly learned, they have to be lived, expressed and found desirable. This experiencing of values helps substantially to define the role of higher education, for its role is designed to interpret these symbols operationally and enthusiastically to enhance their necessary contribution to individual and social living. Education exists, I repeat, to bring each person into an awareness of and participation in the realizing of the best of these humanly prized, historically tested aspirations and activities.

How absolute each individual finds these values to be, is in the first instance, a matter of his own judgment and his own background of education. But it is my own profound conviction that we find in human experience that the mandate to achieve, to struggle to realize values of a progressively qualitative character, is an absolute and not a relative demand which life makes upon us. Thus it is that education as public and as social—and there is, in this deeper sense, no private education—is intrinsically a moral enterprise. Its effective pursuit is a moral imperative upon teacher and student, no less than upon the society which requires it. We have not only the moral obligation to be intelligent, but also an obligation to use that intelligence to the utmost extent possible in creating conditions that make for the good life for individuals and for society.

The good life is progressively understood only as we consciously study to understand it. Only thus does it become true that the Kingdom of God on Earth or the Kingdom of Righteousness are revealed as values, as supplying claims which are at once the means and the ends of human endeavor. The approach to higher education through this obligation to achieve values is a moral pursuit pervading every aspect and effort within the educational process. It is thus true that nothing educationally valued can escape analysis, criticism, reinforcement, and the further creative elaboration which it is education's task to supply.

In short, education, intrinsically, has no secular role. It can be secular only where it is selfish, self-centered, complacent, or indifferent about the valuable, which means acquiescent in a moral neutrality. Education is society organized to advance the capacity and the desire of its members to be rational, productive, loving, and reverential. To be rational, to be creative, to be loving, to be reverent—these are ultimate values higher education is committed to cherish. And in this special sense, education is committed to a task which is close to and contributory to that of high religion.

We come now to the final question as to the possible ways of relating this conception of high religion to the ordinary practices of education itself. How is the effectiveness of education to be strengthened and purified in the light of the absolute mandate made upon individuals to be committed to a certain way of life?

First, there are certain historically unique complications and urgencies about this problem of which explicit account has to be taken. I refer here to the threats to the human values of Western civilization imposed by the philosophy and momentary objectives of the totalitarian countries. There has been a shocking revival of the view that the person is only a means to the ends of the state; that cruelty, hatred, and murder are allowable to advance the ends of the state; and, finally, that our kind of democracy is to be ridiculed and dismissed as a decadent, "imperialistic capitalism."

Confronted by this drastic denial of our own basic values, the problem of sectarian and theological differences at home, while it may not sink into unimportance, becomes one which must not be allowed to destroy the unity of attack within Western civilization upon the heresies of totalitarianism. Can we, whether Protestants, Jews, Catholics, Mohammedans, or of any other group, afford today the luxury of division in our ranks? On behalf of programs of friendly communication among ourselves and persistent efforts to maintain friendly communication with others with whom we differ, our striving has to be a united one. We have to find shared and common bases of collaboration. Clearly, all this will not be done on a theological level, and we should waste valuable time if we should attempt to do this. At some point, and the sooner the safer, we must come to see that the godlike yearning for non-violence, for human fraternity, requires a concentration of strategy at least equal to a yearning for theological clarity.

We shall never go back to "first principles" in the sense that this phrase is so often used. We shall never again enjoy the luxury of complete agreement. We must settle for a diversity of theologies, but we must also settle for a unity of values in a search for areas of agreement in program and devoted commitment to that program. To look out upon our world educationally and religiously, in other words, and to get thought and feeling focused through education upon a grasp of the ways to human unity, is not only an imperative assignment, but it is one in which high religion and education virtually merge in their interest and their common responsibility.

In the second place, our colleges confront the practical problem of the more careful scrutiny of the credentials of the new teacher. And I do not, of course, mean denominational credentials. Rather we want responsible, ethically sensitive, morally alive, and spiritually alert men and women in the positions of college teaching, irrespective of the formal affiliations they may or may not have.

We want to avoid a virtual repudiation by teachers of the deeper meanings of the spiritual heritage of the Western world; to avoid a caustic skepticism or bland agnosticism or aggressive atheism. We want some recognition that although the scientific road to truth is important and must be protected, clarified, and extended, it is not the only road to spiritual insight and wisdom. We want teachers who have a committed love of truth seeking, of truth finding, of "standing and having done all, to stand" for what they believe, as a professional requirement.

And then, as integral to the character of the teachers, we must try increasingly to assure that always, in every course, beyond the considerations of fact, there is explicit consideration of the ways and means of reaching defensible value judgments. The American college tends on the whole to be supersaturated with the aim of imparting facts as ultimate, with no adequate consideration by teachers and students together as to their meaning, their value, their comparative importance in helping to illuminate decisions upon present human issues.

Education, properly conceived, is carried on with what Eduard C. Lindeman has called a *moral bias;* and what someone else has called a *pervasive ethical thrust.* But we do not get a moral bias, nor a pervasive ethical thrust, unless we have morally sensitive and ethically alert teachers.

I realize that we cannot change the existing situation completely in the next few years. But until the quality of the personal outlook of American college teachers changes in this more elevated and integrated direction, we will not have religion in our colleges in the sense that I am stressing, because we will still be overburdened with those who suffer from an overdose of skepticism, from an excessive experimentalism, an excessive moral relativism, all of which confuse young people of college age and leave them with few guideposts or standards.

We can do a much better job with the interpretation of spiritual values brought us in the Hebraic-Hellenic contributions to our great

Western tradition. We have not been at pains to interpret that whole historic process and pageant in ways that point up their immense value implications for us in the world of today.

We can also do far more than we have with the utilization of the non-academic and non-classroom activity as a further medium and occasion of moral instruction and spiritual interest. This will not be done by preaching, but by upholding standards of excellence; by being assured that all those who are in contact with students in the extracurricular, in the athletic and social affairs, in the conduct of assemblies and chapels, in musical and in dramatic presentations, that all are fine personalities who in spontaneous but profound ways arouse the loyalties and bring about a heightened aspiration on the part of young people.

Far more can be done with this moralizing of the higher educational process if and when sports are conducted with complete integrity as they are *not* in too many colleges; and when our drama and our music are designed not to trivialize, but to enhance the sensitivities of the human spirit.

We have also to strive in every conceivable way to make sure that honesty in the conduct of classwork and of examinations comes to be the only recognized and tolerated standard of decency on the campus. There has been a great wave of dishonesty in examinations in recent years, and if that is to be allowed to go on and is not made a proper concern of sensitive teachers, it bodes ill for any moral or religious outlook of the young people affected by it.

Similarly, with presently prevailing attitudes, including the relative notions of morals held by so many, how the social life of boys and girls at the college age and under college auspices shall be conducted, becomes a genuine problem of moral tone. I have myself shared in enough such occasions with young people to know that unless there is on the part of adult friends an adherence, day in and day out, to standards of excellence and taste, and the holding of young people and their representative leaders to the fulfilling of these standards in the conduct of such affairs, they can deteriorate and disintegrate all too readily. But it does take devoted, committed, loving care by older people who are friends and not "chaperones."

What I have been saying—at least by indirect suggestion—is that the situation of religion in higher education is not an either-or matter. It is not that we have it or do not have it. It is clearly not a case of the presence or absence of instruction emanating from the direct promptings of some organized religious point of view. It is not a matter of advancing that theology which is our own favorite prescription. We all have such prescriptions and such convictions, and they have their value, albeit limited because all of our visions are limited.

Rather I say, in conclusion, as I said at the outset, that we have to reaffirm and clarify at a deeper level of meaning the basic purpose of higher education. This purpose is essentially of a high religious quality even though it has to function in the absence of any consensus about theology.

That seems to me to be the raw and inescapable fact of today and tomorrow. Each person must be allowed, in every public and private college, to clarify his own God-idea and his own language for it. But every teacher *should be* committed to a responsible seeking for the ultimate values, and to moral behavior rationally and scientifically guided through revelations of truth which occur progressively, and through educational enlightenment as to the nature of what is good and true and beautiful.

There must be shared insights and a laying hold upon instrumentalities of a wide variety of frocked and unfrocked persons. Education is the indispensable guidance and illumination of a reverent approach to all experience. As Whitehead has said, "Ignorance has the guilt of vice."

Some will regard my conclusion as the merest interim report, or not even as a report of progress. Some will say I affirm too much for education and too little for religion. Indeed, some may allege that I do not grasp what religion is. Some will say, also, that the religion I suggest is so abstruse or impersonal as to have little or no appeal for college students.

There may be a measure of truth in all such reactions. But one thing I do not believe it permissible to do, and that is to project one's personal belief, faith, and theology upon others as something necessary for their personal fulfilment, despite one's own sense of its desirability.

I would not like to have this interpreted as an appeal to some religious "highest common denominator." I would rather put it that I am seeking a highest common factor of agreement compatible with sincere diversity of conviction, and with the realization, also, of the dire necessity for agreement upon a certain kind of program and performance throughout the Western world. Let there be agreement, as far as possible, that the God many of us gladly accept for authority, support, sanction, and salvation, may still help to supply the plot and the rationale of the human drama.

But if we believe in this kind of God-idea, we can still pursue the labors of higher education earnestly, devotedly, with clear conscience, without any insistence that others accept the verbalized expression of our personal faith.

What we should seek is a linking together of the striving and aspiration of us all for a higher education which elevates the sights and ennobles the values of all who share in the enterprise of learning.

VIII

RELIGION IN A STATE TEACHERS COLLEGE

BY

ROSCOE L. WEST, ED.M.

President, New Jersey State Teachers College at Trenton

In considering the subject which is before us for this particular paper, the first thing which we should do is to ask ourselves, "What are the educational objectives of a State teachers college?" An obvious answer would be that the major aim of a teachers college is to educate teachers. But the question immediately arises, "What does this involve and how is it to be done?"

In many parts of the country State teachers colleges have taken on other obligations besides that of educating teachers. This function, however, is still very important in such colleges and in some parts of the country, particularly in the East, State teachers colleges are still primarily for the purpose of providing teachers for the public schools. Because of this relationship to the public schools they have always been close to the "grass roots" thinking of the American people, and they must, therefore, be responsive to the major convictions of the people and their desires for the transmission of these convictions into the public schools.

The public schools of America exist for all of the children of all the people. They cater to no particular sect or group. It took about two hundred years to proceed from the early idea that education was the province of the church, through the development of the notion that public education was only for "paupers," to our modern concept that it is the responsibility of the state to see that education is provided for all of the children even through the professional schools of the university. The long fight for this concept was not really won until the 1880's.

Perhaps more than any other influence public schools have been responsible for welding our conglomerate heritage into a unit in which groups of vastly different social, cultural, and religious origins and standards can work together peacefully. The undisputed source of anti-democratic thought and action is prejudice. The principal source of prejudice is what the sociologists call ethnocentrism, that is, a feeling that one's own group is superior to other groups. This is the feeling that "we are the *in* group and those not belonging to us are the *out* group." In the United States, where the population is made up of so many diverse groups, the most effective weapon against the development of ethnocentrism has been the public school. Even though factors exist in the home, in the church, or in a fraternal order to promote ethnocentrism, the public school has had the opportunity to counteract the prejudice of the *in* group. Sociologists have pointed out, therefore, that the American school is more than a melting pot. It has taught that it is right to be different, but that differences between groups should be understood without prejudice and absorbed into certain common aims designed for the common good.

Teachers colleges exist in a framework which is peculiar to this country, namely, that of control of schools by the States with practically no pattern setting or controls by the Federal Government. Of course, they must be in tune with the constitutional and statutory provisions, both Federal and State, which affect public policy. Great variations exist between the institutions of different States with respect to standards and types of curricula offered. The American system, though lacking in uniformity, does give opportunity for experimentation. Although one finds it difficult to put his finger on specific practices which one can say are followed all over the country, one can always point to differences in practice which often lead the way to common procedures which may be accepted in later periods.

In defining the objectives of teachers colleges, one must keep in mind that these institutions also share to a certain extent the objectives of all institutions of higher education. To prepare teachers means not only to follow specific objectives relating to the knowledge and skills which a teacher must have in order to function efficiently in a classroom, but it also involves education of persons who will be teachers in accordance with objectives which are generally accepted by institutions of higher education.

During the past twenty-five years one of the most significant developments in American education has been the extension of the education of teachers, elementary as well as secondary, from the limited two-year normal school to a standard four-year post-high school status. While many States cannot under present circumstances enforce this standard for all teachers, the institutional pattern has been built on the four-year basis. Contrary to the apparent opinion of many critics of teacher education, the bulk of the teachers college curriculum is not pedagogical. In fact, many teachers colleges have as much as seventy to seventy-five per cent of their work in the general fields of literature, mathematics, science, social studies, and the arts.

The objectives of higher education can be expressed in a great variety of ways. For the purposes of our discussion, I am using what I consider to be a very clear statement of these objectives made by former President Edmund E. Day of Cornell University in an address given at a national conference of university and college administrators and educators called by the American Council on Education in Washington in October of 1950.[1] In that address Dr. Day pointed out that education "as a social process is expected to transmit the cultural heritage, including the basic social organization and political structure." He then goes on to state that the job of education is "to (1) convey knowledge, (2) develop skills, (3) arouse interest, (4) cultivate habits, (5) impart understanding, and (6) establish ideals." He points out that these objectives are mixed in varying proportions in different types of education. For example, in professional education great emphasis is placed upon the development of skills, whereas in liberal education more emphasis is placed on the gaining of understanding.

During recent years much attention has been given to the problem of "general" education, which I understand to mean the knowl-

[1] Cf. Miller, "Religion in a State University," pp. 103–104.

edge and understandings that every person should possess to be an intelligent member of our society. Should this basic general education include a consideration of the influence of religion on our democratic social order, or should we expect the student to get most of this from the home and the church? Even if he gets specific religious loyalties from the latter two, is there a role which the school should play in presenting historical, comparative, and perhaps critical data concerning the relation of religion to social development? Can this be done in a public institution or must it be left to institutions not under public control and financing? Public institutions are subject to attack by groups that feel offended by presentation of material that seems inimical to them.

To answer such questions as these for State teachers colleges one must examine their particular objectives and the framework in which they operate. I should certainly subscribe to the idea that teachers colleges must have a proper balance of the objectives listed above for all education, and that certainly the development of understandings and the establishment of ideals is of just as much importance as the development of skills.

Within the framework of the general objectives of all institutions in higher education one can state the more specific objectives of a teachers college under four rather definite headings:

(1) It is the business of a teachers college to give its graduates an adequate general education in the fields of knowledge which are now considered to be essential to any well educated person. Certainly he should have accurate knowledge and understanding of the kind of world in which he lives, the problems of that world at the present time, and he should have developed those interests and ideals which are thought to be customary for an educated person. His interests should be wide and varied. Avoiding jingoism, he should be able to interpret to youth the ideological and economic conflicts of our time and help them to see the contribution which they can make toward the achievement of world stability and peace.

(2) He must have systematic knowledge, understanding, interests, etc., in the particular field where he will teach. The secondary school teacher of science and mathematics, for example, must be adequately

prepared in these fields, and this, of course, applies to all other fields which are to be handled by the teacher.

(3) He must have a knowledge of children—the way in which they grow and develop, how they learn, and what their interests are. He must also know a reasonable amount concerning accepted methods of teaching and those things which are usually thought of as the pedagogical skills of his profession. Before leaving the teachers college he should have a "safety minimum" in teaching skill which he can improve by teaching.

(4) He should have the personality and character traits which are necessary for him in his particular profession. Quite frequently teachers fail because of the lack of these personality traits, and it is sometimes assumed that they are of more importance than skills. It seems to be demonstrable that some persons of high intellectual attainments do not have personality traits which would make them efficient teachers, and apparently a few persons with rather mediocre intellectual interests can become efficient teachers, particularly at certain levels of teaching, if they have very desirable personality traits and know how to get along with the children. In general, however, it is probably demonstrable that a combination of high intellectual ability and desirable personality traits is possible and is existent in a very large percentage of successful teachers.

These objectives of a teachers college are, of course, directly related to the objectives of the American public school system. Criticism has often been made that in this country we lack clearcut educational objectives and it is probably true that we have not developed such clearcut objectives as have always been evident in European school systems. One of the reasons for this vagueness is that we have developed the cosmopolitan, instead of the one-purpose high school. In such a school pupils with a variety of purposes follow common as well as individual objectives, so that the entire school cannot be easily catalogued. We can probably not point to such a clearcut objective as that of turning out the disciplined type of gentleman which has been the aim of the English "public" schools for so many years. Yet it is evident, even in the variety of educational systems in this country, that we do have a common end of our educational process in that we offer wide opportunities for individuals and at the same time develop persons who have an understanding of American democracy and the traits of character which will enable them to meet problems which this democracy now faces. Certainly it cannot be said that American public schools have neglected elements of character education and of development of ideals. They are not godless as has sometimes been said. In some ways they have been far above the surrounding environment in their exemplification of high standards. Schools everywhere emphasize moral and ethical principles.

These principles, however, have been taught without specific religious reference. Some people would, in fact, maintain that good behavior is caught and not taught and that the character of the teacher is much more important than moralistic or religious instruction. Even though such instruction is not given directly by the school, the question arises whether or not an understanding teacher can be produced without having him understand the religious basis of morality. Daniel L. Marsh, Chancellor of Boston University, says, "Any education is morally threadbare which leaves its students unaware of the irreconcilable divergence between good and evil, freedom and necessity, love and self-centeredness, spirit and matter, person and mechanism, progress and stagnation." There are many thinkers in education today who believe deeply that religion cannot be safely left out of the educational process. They point out that American democracy rests upon the biblical doctrines of the sacred worth of human personality, the equality of human rights, brotherhood as interpreted by the Golden Rule, and service as the standard of greatness. Are not these concepts derived from the Judeo-Christian tradition? Should they not be recognized as fundamental religious principles not dependent on any sectarian interpretation?

Dr. George F. Zook, in his last annual report as President of the American Council on Education, has this to say about the problem:

The decline in the recognition of religious values and concepts in the schools and colleges from their earlier dominant position relative to the purpose of education accounts in no small degree for the vacuum and confusion in education which persists to this present day. Particularly it accounts for that period in our educational history when the pursuit of knowledge for its own sake and the worship of subject matter became by default the end of all education. It was a natural consequence of a situation which reflects credit neither on the educators nor the ministers of religion . . . the values and qualities of religion and democracy respectively are so similar and interrelated that they ought to be regarded by educators, by ministers of religion, and by the public as partners in perfecting the individual. It seems, indeed, both illogical and foolish for either to take a neutral attitude toward the other.[2]

Others, however, believe that these understandings must be secured in the home and church and that religion of any sort should be kept out of the public schools. The recent White House Conference on Child Welfare after sharp debates adopted a resolution which said, "we recognize that nothing is of greater importance than the work of religious education in our homes and churches." But, they voted, "we are unalterably opposed to the use of public schools directly, or indirectly, for religious instruction."

In all of the various formulations of the objectives for the public schools I do not recall one that does not emphasize the element of the development of ethics or character. From the expression of objectives in the cardinal principles of education many years ago, down to the publications of the Educational Policies Commission, ethical ideals and character education have been stressed. The publication of the Educational Policies Commission, entitled "The Purposes of Education in American Democracy," pointed out that educational objectives depend on a scale of values and are rooted in the life of a people. A definition of what is good or ethical or worthy goes very deeply into the values which are accepted by the people. When we speak of "character," obviously we are referring to a certain mode of behavior which we think of as good. I do not believe that we can get away from the fact that the type of definition which we accept is rooted in the Hebraic-Christian teachings and tradition.

We have been influenced very little by the ideals of other cultures. In dealing with the Asiatic cultures we are apt to forget that we

---

[2] George F. Zook, "The President's Annual Report," *The Educational Record*, The American Council on Education, Washington, D.C., 1950, pp. 165 f.

have been deeply steeped in the traditions of Hebraic morality and Greek logic. Consequently we sometimes fail to understand that the Asiatic peoples can arrive at a solution of a problem which seems ethical to them and unethical and unreasonable to us. If we are constantly to be close with all peoples of the world, we shall have to seek to understand better both our own value system and the systems of other cultures. In the interplay of ideas there may then be mutual advantage rather than conflict.

In the objectives of public education as expressed by the Educational Policies Commission, four divisions are made, namely, the objectives of (1) self-realization, (2) human relationship, (3) economic efficiency, and (4) civic responsibility. Under the objective of self-realization the one relating to character is expressed as follows: "The educated person gives responsible direction to his own life." Comment on this is to the effect that:

The development of a philosophy of life, or a religion, is based on the learning process. Like other learning, it is not fully consummated until it makes a difference in the practical conduct of one's life. No imposition of the thinking of another, however well fortified with threats and promises, can give the individual a ready-made philosophy, or a set of superior values. Any other mode than following the processes of education through their natural course of questioning, testing, and forming judgments, is poorly suited to self-realization through democratic processes.

There are certain basic assumptions in connection with our public schools which should perhaps be stated as we proceed with the discussion of the problem of religion in State institutions such as State teachers colleges. We need to remind ourselves that the United States of America is committed to a policy of religious freedom. The principles of religious liberty are embodied in the Constitution and the Bill of Rights. We are also committed to a policy of public responsibility for education. All children who do not attend parochial or privately supported schools must go to schools provided and administered, financed and supported by the state and its subdivisions.

We are fairly clear in our understanding that the Constitution of the United States, particularly as amended by the First and Fourteenth Amendments, has established a very definite policy that there shall not be any "establishment of religion" in this country, either by the Federal Government or by the States. We have spoken of this policy as "separation of church and state." Yet we do not seem to have developed a clear conception of what this separation means. Does it mean no religion in a public school, that is, no religious exercises? Obviously we have not so interpreted it, because nearly all of the States of the Union permit and some require the reading of the Bible in public schools. Does the principle of separation of church and state mean that there will be no singing of religious hymns or celebration of religious holidays in the schools? Obviously not, because these practices are carried on in most of the schools of the country, and the basis of such observances seems to be on a sufficiently common ground of spiritual understanding so that no serious objection has been made by any particular sect which does not itself actively participate in these celebrations.

The separation of church and state has come to mean that we recognize no religion as a state religion. We have no recognized clerical party. The state may make no laws prohibiting the free exercise of religion. On the other hand, we recognize the validity of non-taxation of church property, which means that the state is taking a hand in encouraging religion. Where State constitutions permit the use of public funds for auxiliary service to parochial schools in the form of free transportation and free secular textbooks, the state is giving aid (indirectly, it is true, but aid nevertheless) to the furtherance of religion. Released-time programs for religious instruction again indicate that the lines of separation between church and state are changing. Although the Supreme Court has emphasized the demarcation by ruling that public school buildings may not be used for religious teaching, we do not yet know whether the cooperation of church and state in other aspects of the program is a violation of the separation doctrine. Nor can we be sure that all future Supreme Courts will rule as the present one has.[1]

We have accepted the general principle that there should be no sectarian teaching in the public schools, but we have not explored to

[1] See pp. 188 f. Ed.

any extent the areas of common agreement on fundamental spiritual values so that these items can be handled intelligently. The proposal of the committee of the American Council on Education that religion should be studied as a part of the culture, and that it can be handled objectively as a controversial issue just as items in politics or economics are treated, is an extremely intriguing view. There are probably more difficulties in the proposal than appear on the surface. We have become accustomed to political and social controversy and have, on the whole, developed a willingness to allow all points of view to be presented. The basis of this is the acceptance of the idea that truth is arrived at through study, discussion, argument, and even controversy. Religion, however, is not considered by most people as a *search for truth,* but as acceptance of certain truth previously established and having divine sanction. To handle discussions in this field requires a teacher more broadly and objectively trained than to handle controversial questions in the social sciences.

One can advocate high tariff or low tariff, income taxes or sales taxes, centralization of government or states rightism without being thought of as a dangerous person. But even in political differences of opinion there are limits. One may not advocate "Communism," as such a doctrine is considered subversive of our fundamental political framework. Even to try to teach *about* Communism is a dangerous procedure. Not too many years ago a federal statute forbade any mention of Russia in the schools of the District of Columbia. Apparently the lawmakers felt that any knowledge of what they regarded as evil would tend to corrupt the youth. Evil was to be abolished by assuming that it did not exist, instead of by studying it to find out how inferior it was to the American system which was thought of as "good." Current investigations demonstrate how easily one may be accused of being a "Communist" and barred from useful public service.

There have been many instances in recent years of objections to textbooks used in the schools because some of the material was critical of American mores and of our social and economic status. Some such books have been labeled "un-American" and have been voted out of schools by school boards. There are many people who do not believe that pupils can consider various points of view concerning a given social problem and thus arrive at an opinion which is backed by critical thinking. They might admit that American social and political life is not perfect, but they still wish to have it taught to the young as the "best" in the world.

To be sufficiently scholarly and objective in the field of religion to present its different points of view, is even more difficult than in the political and social realm. American public opinion is not inclined to consider it wise to subject the young to teaching that might extol the merits of religions other than Christianity. And within Christianity, very few teachers would consider themselves capable of presenting accurately the beliefs of different sects on various theological doctrines.

One may wonder, for example, what would happen in some communities if a teacher said that some of the Bible is poetry, much is symbolic rather than literally true, many of the books were written many years after the actual events took place, and are, therefore, inaccurate. Such a person might well be called a "dangerous and subversive" person, undermining the faith of young people. Until the churches get a common understanding of what religion is and how its literature should be interpreted, the public school trying to handle this material is in a ticklish situation.

Even in presenting the religious conflicts involved in history, such as occurred in Europe at the time of the Reformation, there are difficulties. Not long ago one State department of education requested the teachers colleges not to use a certain book as a textbook because of complaints made to the department concerning the treatment of the medieval religious controversies. The author had used critical language concerning both sides of the controversy but this did not assuage the hurt feelings of those allied to one group. A revised edition of the book in which criticisms were softened was later approved.

Because the graduates of State teachers colleges go directly to the public schools to teach children, the public is more sensitive to what happens in these institutions than it is to the program of a State university. Some of these problems may be responsible for the fact that, in general, State teachers colleges have paid less attention to religion than State universities.

These difficulties may explain why teachers colleges have not pioneered in this field. To date there has been little demand from the public that they exert leadership or even experiment to any extent. They have, on the whole, stayed on the safe side. Not many studies have been made to find out exactly what is being done and even those that have been reported are very limited in scope.

The American Association of Teachers Colleges through a sub-committee of the Committee on Standards and Surveys made a study of religious practices and interest which was reported in the 1947 Yearbook of that association. Replies were received from approximately 150 of the 185 members of the association. A number of interesting conclusions are pointed out in the report of the committee.

Although fifty-seven colleges encouraged denominational meetings, seventy-five actually discouraged these meetings. In all, 108 reported encouragement of interdenominational meetings, but twenty-nine even discouraged this type of religious activity.

Sixty-two schools reported the observance of some type of "religious week," whereas eighty-three reported no such observance, and thirty-three said they are not interested in having such a week.

Ninety-five schools offered no courses which could be named as courses in religion or in the Bible.

Eighty-three colleges reported some type of denominational groups but sixty-six reported none.

One astonishing finding was to the effect that at the regular assembly programs only twenty-four reported that the Bible was ordinarily read, whereas 116 said that this was not the case. One hundred and twenty-two institutions reported that prayer was not a regular part of assembly programs.

One hundred and seventeen made no provision for a daily devotional service as compared with twenty-eight that reported such provision.

One hundred and thirty-one offered no type of special training for Sunday school teachers or other religious education and seventy-seven said they would oppose such courses.

Whereas eighty-one reported some form of systematic effort to get students to attend church, fifty-eight did absolutely nothing about this. Thirteen of these fifty-eight said that there would be serious objection in their communities to any program designed to sponsor church attendance.

Only thirty-eight had a faculty committee designed to encourage and supervise extra-instructional religious activities.

Thirty-seven reported special showings of motion pictures of religious nature, contrasted with 103 that do not have such showings.

Forty-two provide space for the use of outside religious organizations. One hundred and four do not. Of these latter, fifty-eight do not think it would be desirable and thirty are in doubt.

The committee remarked that "one gets the impression of caution from analyzing responses to the inquiry. The administrators seem to feel that they are teetering near a precipice in these fields."

On the other hand, it was reported that 134 have a baccalaureate sermon, 143 use ministers in the commencement program, 126 bring outstanding religious leaders to the campus to address students, 110 provide some form of special opportunity for ministers to make contacts with students, 122 supply churches with names of students who prefer these churches, and 109 report that local ministers are invited to appear before student bodies.

The committee concluded:

. . . religious practices in the state teachers colleges lag far behind the religious interests of the administrations of the colleges. In still other terms, it would appear that there is indisputable evidence of religious interests in the vast majority of these colleges but that religious practices and procedures tend to be desultory and restricted, unsystematic, if not even timorous in form of expression. As previously indicated, it would seem that this discrepancy between interest and practice emanates from the American philosophy of separation between church and state, and the related notion in popular thinking that religious activity and instruction are synonymous with denominational activity and instruction. Faced with these two hurdles, there appears to be a very real tendency for the colleges to "play the game safely," and, in the main, develop only enough of a religious program to appease those with outstanding religious interests while not offending those with any particular sectarian bent.[3]

A more recent study was reported in the *North Central Association Quarterly* of January, 1950. It was entitled "Teaching of Religion and Philosophy in Sixty-Five (State) Teachers Colleges in North Central Territory," and was made by Dean O. T. Richardson of Ball State Teachers College, Muncie, Indiana. By a check of the catalogues of the sixty-five institutions involved, it was reported that forty per cent offer courses in religion, thirty-one per cent in philosophy, and fifty-four per cent in either religion or philosophy. The largest number of semester hours offered in religion was fifteen and one half at the Southwest Missouri State Teachers College at Springfield. Only one institution (Black Hills, South Dakota) indicated that a course in religion was required for graduation: according to the catalogue a course entitled, "Introduction to Philosophy," or "The World's Great Religions," will be required of seniors graduated in 1950 and thereafter. Three teachers colleges reported that a field of concentration may be worked out in either religion or philosophy (Northeast Missouri State Teachers College, Indiana State Teachers College, and Central Missouri State Teachers College). The general conclusion of the study is as follows:

It would seem logical that the teaching of religion and philosophy in State Teachers Colleges would need to be based on a particular need for courses of this character, as for any other course in the college curriculum. It could be argued that courses in these two fields would contribute appreciably (1) to the general education of students, (2) to the general culture of students, (3) towards giving a framework or meaning to the why's and wherefore's of life, or (4) to provide training that will be useful for future teachers. One State Teachers College states that "The purpose of the Bible course is to give a student a definite and organized knowledge of the contents of the English Bible, in order that its historical, literary, and spiritual value may be fully appreciated and may become a useful tool in character building. The purpose of the Religious

[3] William H. Vaughn, Paul L. Garrett and Paul L. Boynton, "Religious Practices in State Teachers Colleges," *Twenty-sixth Yearbook,* American Association of Teachers Colleges, A department of the National Education Association, Washington, D.C., 1947, pp. 115, 116.

Education courses is to help ministerial students and others to become more effective preachers and Sunday School teachers."

The broadened curriculum in State Teachers Colleges today includes much pre-professional work which can be compared to the so-called "liberal education" received in the private liberal arts colleges. Most of the private liberal arts colleges offer courses in either religion or philosophy. It may be that State Teachers Colleges, in their transition from straight teacher training to a curriculum including more pre-professional work, may wish to add these courses to enable their graduates to compare more favorably with the products of the private liberal arts colleges.

It would appear necessary to prove that students should have these disciplines in order to become better trained teachers. Research on this point is not conclusive enough to draw valid conclusions.

Since the material for this study was secured from the college catalogues of the State Teachers Colleges in the North Central area, the reader should realize that what is oftentimes so announced is not always carried out. It would be advisable to request additional information from the State Teachers Colleges which list courses in either religion or philosophy.[4]

These two studies are very partial in their scope, and an examination of the items covered would indicate that a much more comprehensive study would have to be made to ascertain all of the places in the curricula and in the life of the school in which religion or spiritual values are considered. A rather informal contact with several teachers colleges indicates to me that such a comprehensive study would show that there are many courses in teachers colleges in which some phase of religion or religious history is touched.

Inasmuch as the subject which I was requested to discuss was stated as "Religion in a State Teachers College," I am assuming that it will be proper and interesting to give a brief report of religious activities at the college with which I am familiar, namely, the New Jersey State Teachers College at Trenton. This college, like many other teachers colleges reported in the study of the American Association of Teachers Colleges, has not offered any specific courses in

[4] O. T. Richardson, "Teaching of Religion and Philosophy in Sixty-five Teachers Colleges in North Central Territory," *North Central Association Quarterly,* Ann Arbor, January, 1950.

religion or in philosophy dealing with religious themes. It has, however, dealt with phases of this problem in many ways, and I believe it can be said that it has encouraged the development of spiritual values.

In the weekly assembly, which is required of all students, the Bible is usually read, the Lord's Prayer is used, and sometimes a hymn is sung. It has been the object of the administration to use some types of prose and poetry other than the Bible to demonstrate that they have spiritual significance. In connection with the assembly, every year or two a representative of the Jewish Chautauqua Society has addressed the students on the Hebraic background as it relates to our current society. For years the Thanksgiving and Christmas assemblies have been of religious type, with music by the choir and an address by Dean Robert Wicks of Princeton University Chapel. These addresses have been aimed to present spiritual values as of universal concern and have made the services outstanding in their tone and significance.

On the evening before students go home for Thanksgiving recess, all of the women of the college have for years had a "Priscilla Procession" in connection with dinner in which, dressed in the Priscilla costume of the Pilgrims, they file into their places, using the psalms sung by the Pilgrims in Plymouth. At Christmastime, in addition to usual celebrations, the College Choir gives a Sunday afternoon concert of religious music which is attended by over a thousand students and friends.

The college bus is made available on Sundays for those who wish to go to Trenton, five miles away, to religious services. Two or three church bodies have established groups on the campus, although these have not been encouraged, as it has been the attitude of the administration that unifying religious programs should be encouraged and that students should go to their respective churches in the surrounding community for the individual religious experience which they desire to have.

The Chapter of Kappa Delta Pi, which is an honor society in teachers colleges and schools of education, chose as its program during a recent year a study of religion in the community. As a part of this study, visits were made to a Protestant church, to a Catholic church, and to a Jewish synagogue, with presentation and discussion by the religious leaders in these groups. Several denominations were represented in the group, and at the end of the year the chapter felt that it had had a very interesting and profitable consideration of this topic.

A contribution from the Danforth Foundation has also made it possible for one member of the faculty to act as casual adviser to students in religious matters.

A baccalaureate sermon is always a part of commencement activities. One of the features of commencement is a presentation by a student selected by faculty and the senior class of a subject selected by him. It is interesting to note that not long ago the student chose to discuss the problem of religion in education as her commencement speech. The gist of her argument was for a greater emphasis on religion in the public schools than we now have.

Although no specific courses in religion are offered, the subject is considered in many courses. In the freshman course in "Rise of Contemporary Civilization," a unit of three weeks duration is devoted to the "Rise of Dominant Religions in the Western World." In this unit such topics as the following are considered: Trends in Judaism, The Beginnings of Christianity, The Triumph of Christianity in the Roman Empire, The Rise of Islam, The Spread of Islam.

In the course in "World Literature" which is now required of all sophomores, the Bible or some part of it is one of the units of the course. In this course at least five core books are used, one of which is the Bible. Certain instructors assign all of the First and Second Books of Samuel, as well as the Gospel According to Matthew. In other classes certain other books of both the Old and the New Testament are read. During the current year certain instructors in this course are using a book called *The World Bible,* which includes selections from the Bible, the Koran, Confucius, and other religious books. Here there is a definite attempt to present religious philosophy other than the Hebraic-Christian and to get a world view of religious thought.

Several films presenting Christianity and the religions of China and the Moslem world have been previewed. It was decided that none of the films was suitable for class use. Criticism of the films was to the effect that the photography was poor and that they were for the most part on a very simple level. This department felt that there is a definite need for adequate film material in the field of religion.

One instructor reports that there is a definite attempt to present three world ethical religious systems to form a background of values against which various literary works may be studied. The first system, the philosophy of Confucius, is presented through the Modern Library text translated by Lin Yutang. The second system of ethics, the Greek system, is presented through the writings of Plato and some of Sophocles and Euripides. The third system, the Judeo-Christian, is explored through readings from the King James Bible "which is abridged and designed to be read as literature." Attention is especially called to the humanity of the Bible, its universal appeal, and its dramatic and poetic values. Throughout this course the emphases are on the literary contributions of religion, as well as on the effect of religion on the emotions and thinking of the human race. Applied to such books as Hawthorne's *The Scarlet Letter* and Stone's *Lust for Life,* the value of such religious and ethical background is obvious.

In the course in sociology required of all juniors, no attempt is made to deal with religion as a separate topic, but every possible opportunity is utilized to treat it in incidental fashion. Concepts which are emphasized are as follows:

1. Religion is shown to be a universal factor in all cultures.
2. Religion is a significant force in all primitive and folk cultures, and seems to suffer a loss of influence in technological societies.
3. Cultures swing from the sacred to the secular in some sort of pattern. The effects of secularization are carefully noted.
4. Attention is given to the church as a social institution, an agency of social control, and a source of social reform.
5. Variations in religious behavior in relation to race, nationality, and social class are analyzed.
6. The relation of religion to social policy is stressed. For ex-

ample, population control, educational policy, and similar social issues are shown to be affected by religious belief.

7. The relation of religion to community welfare and the improvement of attitudes of various groups in the community toward one another are given consideration.

8. Illustrations of social processes are often chosen in terms relevant to religion. The process of accommodation, for example, is illustrated by the work of the National Conference of Christians and Jews.

9. Religious groups are chosen to illustrate types of social organization. For example, the Catholic Church illustrates the vertical type of social group.

10. Some attention is given to the role of values in the structuring of personality. As many of these values are religious, it is necessary to note them as such.

11. In considering the family, the change from sacrament to contract is stressed. The decline of religious function of the family is noted. The work done by churches in the field of marital conciliation is mentioned.

12. There is some discussion of the relation of religion to juvenile delinquency.

13. In discussing the problem of the disturbed personality, there are frequent references to the function of religion, such as the psychiatric effects of the confessional.

14. The topic in which religion looms the largest is that of intergroup tensions. Specific attention is given to competition and conflict between Catholic, Protestant, and Jewish groups in America. Some time is also devoted to the discussion of denominational tensions.

Courses in history of education pay some attention to the religious background of our educational system and the part that religion played in early schools which preceded the modern practices of free public education. This is also discussed briefly in certain of the "education" courses. In school law the statutes of the State in which the school is located relating to religious observance are considered and in the courses in American government attention is given to the constitutional provisions relating to religion and the separation of church and state.

These represent the major ways in which items concerning religion are touched in the college curricular and extracurricular activities.

The material from the two general studies quoted and the brief discussion of activities at the Trenton State Teachers College indicate that perhaps more than is commonly understood, general religious and spiritual values are being achieved in many teachers colleges. It is perhaps true that the program would vary greatly among colleges, and that there is not a clearcut conception of exactly what results are to be expected. It would also appear that teachers colleges do not give organized personal guidance in religious thinking to students which is available at many private colleges and even at State universities. I am not aware of any teachers college that has a resident minister and very few have chapels which are dedicated to religious activities.

It can certainly be said that teachers colleges are seriously concerned to graduate prospective teachers who have high ethical and spiritual standards. They are a part of the common American society and share this society's concern, whatever it is, for the development of an approved kind of character. It should not be expected that they will be very much different from the society in which they exist. Their objectives will in the long run depend on the desires of the people in the development of the general public school system. If the people are convinced that the schools can and should give more attention to fundamental religious values than has been done in the past, the teachers colleges can take a significant part in this program. For the most important element in such a program would be the teacher. She must have a broad, intelligent concept of the purposes of religious emphasis and be so well grounded herself that she can understand what the school can do and what it should leave to other auspices.

Clearly, there should be a partnership in this phase of education between the home, church, and school. Here is where much research is needed to determine just what phases of the program should be undertaken by each member of the partnership. Furthermore, the teachers college is dependent on the general colleges, universities, and graduate schools of education for the preparation of its teachers, and unless it can secure persons who are themselves objectively and thoroughly competent to handle questions which go to the root of the ethical basis of our society, then the program cannot be carried on successfully.

Society itself must look at the school as less of a place where predetermined truths are taught to the youth, and more of a place where the young are led to discover for themselves the values of life which seem to be valid and capable of standing the tests of experience. This is by no means the idea that many people have of the school today, and those who attempt to live by the more liberal, critical formula are apt to find themselves in difficulty, because they will be accused of not being loyal to those truths which the members of the dominant groups in society think should be inculcated.

The issues of our day, however, are moral issues and the teachers colleges of the country should not evade these issues. They have a dominant role to play in producing the kind of teacher who understands the problems of our time and has the equipment to stand in the forefront of the ranks of those who would prepare Americans to meet these issues valiantly and wisely. It is evident that our world today is in ferment and that new methods are bound to be tried to meet new problems. Much exploration and study are needed of the ways by which our society can improve the understandings of youth of the spiritual and moral values which should guide our actions. As new patterns are developed, the teachers colleges should participate boldly in experimentation, so that we may determine what our society can do to keep the liberties which we prize and at the same time achieve the commonly accepted standards which will be guides to personal and social conduct.

IX

RELIGION IN PRIVATELY SUPPORTED
HIGHER EDUCATION

BY

MILDRED McAFEE HORTON, LL.D.

Formerly President, Wellesley College

The difference between privately and publicly supported institutions of higher education with respect to religion is that in our privately supported institutions the teaching of religion is theoretically and legally permissible. I take for granted that it is theoretically desirable—if for no other reason than on the strictly secular premise that religion, and specifically the Jewish-Christian heritage, is a significant aspect of our culture.

There are practical difficulties in relating religion to higher education, which arise from the nature of religion and from the nature of academic institutions. Look first at the very essential facts about religion. Religion as we know it involves certain convictions, the experience of worship, and resultant action. I should think that it would be theoretically easy to incorporate into an educational program a defined, dogmatic religion in a college or university administered by an institution of that faith. An authority can prescribe the convictions to be taught, can define the forms of worship and the appropriate action to be taken in the name of the religion. I have to speak from the position of a person whose experience has been in the Protestant tradition and in its least authoritarian branches. To maintain a Protestant college, which is non-dogmatic and non-sectarian, at once involves providing for freedom to maintain contradictory convictions, for varieties of worship experience, and for liberty to act on the basis of personal conviction of right and wrong. To the believer and the unbeliever this results in a program closely akin to secularism.

Let me formulate my own prejudices growing out of a very specialized type of experience. My chief experience with relating religion to higher education has of course been at Wellesley College. This college was founded by an ardent convert to Evangelical Christianity "for the glory of God through the service of our Lord Jesus Christ." It was marked originally by all the insignia of nineteenth century evangelism—Bible study, Sabbath observance, missionary activity, prayer groups, required attendance at chapel. The founder embarrassed youngsters periodically by asking them, publicly and privately, about the state of their souls. To the modern educator, however profoundly interested in religion, that sounds quaint and a bit stuffy. But nobody at the time the college was founded doubted that it was a Christian college. Everybody said so and everybody knew it.

There is a difference now; the trustees still say so; the by-laws of the college retain the phrase; the faculty must be selected with a view to maintaining the Christian character of the college; and it is still required that sophomores shall study "the sacred Scriptures." Chapel was long since unrequired, though it is provided daily and well attended. But I am reasonably sure that there are students, and probably some members of the faculty, who would never think of the college as a Christian college. Many would be glad to have it so designated; many would, in the name of liberalism, deplore such designation.

The student body is selected with no reference to ecclesiastical convictions or affiliations, and includes girls of a variety of faiths. Faculty selection involves enough inquiry about religious attitudes to assure respect for those who choose to maintain religious practices on the campus, but there is no general test of religious conviction, and many of the most influential professors are unwilling to identify themselves in any way as affiliated with or even interested in Christianity. The new president of Wellesley told me that certain faculty members had told her with great satisfaction that nobody ever inquires about religious convictions in connection with new appointees. As a matter of fact, it was one of the things I always investigated, but without making it a matter of emphasis. Apparently I did it so casually that it made no impression on my colleagues and thus left the college vulnerable to the charge of secular indifference to religion in faculty appointments.

When the Commonwealth of Massachusetts was proposing the existing legislation on anti-discrimination in selection of students for admission to colleges, our discussions at the college revealed the fact that the omission of any ecclesiastical descriptions on our admission application blanks seemed to many of our liberal faculty members entirely justified, and I was led to believe that in their judgment the religious affiliation of students was literally irrelevant in determining anything about those girls. The liberalism expressed in those discussions of anti-discriminatory legislation was very closely akin to secularism.

If this be true on the college campus, it is simply a reflection of the situation in American society. Our nation was founded in the Christian tradition. The Jewish-Christian heritage is warp and woof of our cultural pattern and has become so much a part of it that much of our secular practice is now identified with our national policy with no reference to its religious heritage.

For example, brotherhood is stylish now among strictly secular intelligentsia. We talk about the significance of the individual as the essence of Western democracy. "Right will prevail over might" is maintained by many good citizens who have no conscious conviction of God's righteous power as the source of their respect for right. Humanitarianism—child welfare, social security—these are logical outgrowths of the Christian conviction, but are accepted now as a part of our secular American society. The Christian citizen, then, does not act very differently from the secular citizen. Scores of men and women interested in social welfare and international goodwill support projects originated by Christians with no awareness of their religious origin.

In an idealistic and humanitarian society religion has been traditionally associated with taboos and obligations. "Thou shalt not" marked the ecclesiastical experience of a good many families. Church obligations were duties, grudgingly performed, whereas civic responsibilities were privileges. To youngsters coming into college the church has been associated frequently with restrictive obligations differentiating them from other young people. This smacked of narrowness, bigotry, intolerance. The emancipation of adolescence involved freedom from adult imposed obligation. Failure to observe the obligation left a sense of guilt, which made traditionalists objectionable as goody-goodies. There was a premium on being good without the fanfare of religious commitment.

These observations are relevant to higher education, because the constituency of American colleges is prevailingly late adolescent. Within our American culture adolescence is characterized by enthusiasm for action, preoccupation with itself and distrust of itself, and transitory experimental commitments to principles. These fall very neatly into the third of our problem areas, which is the liberal arts tradition, where I must talk out of my experience in liberal arts colleges.

The liberal arts tradition is traditional in a rapidly changing society. It is old-fashioned in a new world. And in that old-fashioned status, it finds itself on the defensive. It is accused of irrelevance, of dogmatism, of bigotry, of sentimentality, and the faculties of every liberal arts college are eager to disprove these charges. The liberal arts tradition is associated historically with religious emotionalism, because so many of our colleges were founded in the era of religious emotionalism, and there has been a real confusion in the minds of many people between the fervor of the religious emotionalist and the enthusiasms of the liberal arts tradition. We have tried to absolve ourselves in the academic field from the criticism of sentimentality by avoiding the symptoms of enthusiasm and fervor which go normally along with a healthy religious conviction. The religious conviction, therefore, finds itself out of line and out of sympathy with the characteristic atmosphere of detachment, objectivity, and rationality of the liberal arts tradition.

Young people committed to convictions of any kind are a bit suspect, especially when the conviction includes the religious dynamic which involves the good news of the gospel and fosters missionary motivation. Challenged to submit to ordinary academic examination, religious conviction is wavering. "I believe, help Thou my unbelief," is sissy in academic circles, and what healthy youngster wants to be sissy?

What are the implications of the foregoing observations on a program of religious education in privately supported institutions of higher education? I suggest six.

1. Institutional authorities should identify their position in reference to religion. It is legitimate legally and in every other way for an institution to be neutral or to be sectarian, or to be Protestant and non-sectarian, but I do think it is important for the position of the institution and its official status to be made explicit and clear, so that everyone who enters the college will know what kind of experience he is in for.

2. Religion should be studied academically—not religion in general but the dominant religion of our own culture. In my opinion, the minimum requirement should be acquaintance with the Bible. Whether or not it is a required course should depend, it seems to me, upon the attitude of the institution toward requirements in general. My personal feeling is that so long as the Bible has the place it has in American life, if there are any requirements of any kind it is reasonable to ask students to become acquainted with this book with which so few of them are acquainted when they come to college. That seems to me something that has to be settled, however, within the framework of the particular institution.

It seems logical to provide opportunity for students to know something about the specialized institutions of religion which are important factors in our society. That seems to me relevant even in an institution which has decided to be strictly secular. I wish there were more courses in more American colleges which introduce students to the church with the same degree of enthusiasm with which they introduce students to the American state and to international affairs. The institution of the church is a tremendous factor in our modern life and all too few undergraduates have any reason to know that.

3. I think a college should provide for the practice and demonstra-

tion of worship. If the college has committed itself institutionally to an attitude in relation to religion, it seems to me that its institutional activities should be related to some of the forms of worship. I think it wise to have a daily chapel service, though I think it unreasonable to expect a huge attendance if the service is really optional. Very few of us in adult society go to church every morning before we go to business. I personally like the idea that in connection with the official functions of an academic institution, such as commencement and honors day programs, there should be hymns and prayers, explicit recognition of the fact that this is something other than a purely academic and secular institution. It seems to me that the institution needs to be hospitable to varieties of forms of worship which are perhaps incompatible with the position of the institution itself. In other words, I think it entirely fitting and proper that Catholic students should have an opportunity to worship according to the forms of their faith while they are in residence in a Protestant institution; and if a priest will conduct the Mass in a chapel used by students of other faiths as well, it seems to me desirable that he should do so on a Protestant college campus. I always took satisfaction in the fact that the Episcopal students at Wellesley had a special communion service every week, although the college was not affiliated with the Episcopal church any more than with others.

4. It seems to me that there should be opportunities in a college community for special attention to religion, as there are opportunities for attention to music, to the theater, to politics, to athletics; in other words, forums and conferences which focus the attention of the community on problems of religion and identify this phase of our culture with the problems of education.

5. My personal feeling is that there should be a minimum of pressure for commitment. I like the idea that participation in organizational activities related to religion is encouraged but not pressed. I like the idea that there should be provided plenty of opportunity for theological and ecclesiastical discussions without necessary encouragement to unprepared missionary endeavor. I think that for college students it is good to recognize that identification with Christianity is a privilege to be achieved humbly, and not a duty to be urged upon

recruits. I rather like the idea that the avowed Christians in a college community should think of themselves and be thought of not as "holier than thou," but "happier than thou." I am sure that among young people in an academic community, and probably elsewhere, religious participation should be encouraged by contagion rather than by argument, by example rather than by precept. Clearly all the local practices will have to be adapted to a community custom. Some colleges will have "church" as a regular occasion, a church within the college. On other campuses it is traditional and good practice that students should become part of the congregations of the local churches.

6. Ideally a Christian college, residential in character, is essentially a community of scholars operated throughout on Christian principles. The motivating purpose of its administrators, whether they be trustees, or faculty, or students, differs from that of secular managers in that they are striving to build a community which shall exemplify Christian principles in action. In order to keep that motive vigorous and unsullied, they will maintain a healthy center of refreshment for their own spirits in active worship, seeking God's will for themselves and their college. They are on the record as feeling that their religion matters in the direction of the institution. The whole community is their concern, however, and they are not a group withdrawn from secular life into a religious association. The worship experience is but one phase of the life of a total community committed to the search for truth in conformity to God's will, the dynamo to keep a whole machinery going strong. The academic, social, governmental, athletic, financial, personnel, and recreational policies and programs of the entire college will be subject to standards set by adherence to God's will as nearly as that will can be discovered in honest search for it.

Note that many individuals within the college will be oblivious or possibly skeptical of the religious motivation of avowed Christians who are undertaking to maintain the Christian college. It will not be Christian from the point of view of those who gauge effectiveness of the program by the number of converts. I do not personally visualize the college as a place of religious commitment of many undergraduates, but I consider it to have failed in one important part of its task whenever a student leaves without having gained understanding of and respect for the Christian tradition of our culture. Any student who has made a religious commitment before college should reevaluate it during his college years. I believe his observation of religious activity in college and participation in it should strengthen rather than weaken his commitment, but I am not unduly alarmed if he is not active in Christian work during undergraduate years. It is important for non-Christians and non-Protestants, as well as Protestant students themselves, to be made aware of Protestant values in a Protestant college, without decreased respect for their own commitments.

One question arises insistently about the relation between the church and a college which purports to be a Christian college. I am personally unenthusiastic about the effort of a church to direct a student's religious life, unless the college yields its responsibility and says that it has no program. The approaches of the church and the college are different; both of them are valid, and I personally believe that the church does better to limit its activities on behalf of students to its work in intercollegiate activities where it relates the students of one institution to other institutions, rather than by trying to supplement or substitute something for the work which is being done on the campus in the interest of the students' religious life. My feeling is that the church has a perfectly enormous task in preparing students for their college; but unless a college definitely says that it is not expecting to fulfil any obligation in connection with religious activities of its students, I personally think it is desirable to let the college establish its church program, rather than to expect churches geared to other purposes to be the responsible agents for meeting the religious needs of students while they are in college.

However, this is not to say that the church does not have a major responsibility in connection with students. But I like to put it in these terms.

1. The church is responsible for maintaining such virile and significant religious activity in the community that it cannot be ignored as a phase of our culture.

2. The church can, if it will, capture the enthusiasm of pre-college students for definite identification with the church.

3. It can retain connections with students throughout their stay in college. Just as the home cooperates with the college and maintains tremendous influence over students, so the home church can do great things by encouraging its representatives in the college student body to be pillars in the religious life of the community of which they are now a part; also the church can be sure that when students return home from college they find a welcome and an appropriate place in the church program, so that college young people can feel that they are really needed in the life of the church.

4. The church can offer opportunities for significant participation when young people are seeking jobs and volunteer work. The institution needs the leadership of college-trained young people and ought to have it, but I think it will have to make a great effort just as any business does, to assure a young person that he is really needed upon his return from college.

5. The church can help undergraduates understand the peculiar nature of higher education as a period of inquiry, of tentativeness, of detachment from ordinary responsibility. And by helping them to understand their experience in college while they are observing and becoming so highly critical of their life experience, the church can assist them in reorganizing their experience and promote their re-integration into community life upon their return from college.

X

RELIGION IN A PRIVATELY SUPPORTED SCHOOL OF EDUCATION

SAMUEL L. HAMILTON, PH.D.

Professor of Education, New York University

It was proposed by Dr. Johnson in the opening paper of this series that we are likely to find solutions of the general problem emerging out of concrete situations. Perhaps it would not be amiss for a professor in a New York privately supported school of education to state as simply as he can, what he feels about some of these concrete situations as he has come to know them after twenty years of university teaching.

First of all is the urgency of the present world situation. Individuals and groups and whole blocs of nations are confused and anxious as we enter the second half of the twentieth century. Careful students of the world's cultures find many signs, in the West at least, that we have come to the end of an era of human history. We seem to be at the beginning of a long transition into a different world from that in which Western civilization has enjoyed ascendency unchallenged for four or five centuries.

The citizens of this republic are in a peculiarly trying position. We are literally "on the spot." We are the focal point of the world's attention. We are watched with eager eyes, with hope and expectancy by some, and with open and declared antagonism by others. One hundred and fifty millions of us surrounded by more than two billions of other peoples outside our shores! The free democracies look to us for leadership, for aid, and for protection. The nations of the other bloc are alert to pounce upon our mistakes and failures, because we are seen as a barrier to the spread of their ideology and their rule.

Yet we seem not to be proud of our spotlighted position on the world stage, or happy in it, but worried by it. Perhaps we feel ourselves not quite up to our role. Some long established national policies will have to be changed. Our attitudes will have to become more realistic and responsible—for example, our attitude toward power and coercive force, and toward national sovereignty. A great many American people will have to be changed rather quickly before new policies can be made or accepted. We must learn to commit ourselves to the pursuit of values which are more than individual, more than family, class, race, national, or denominational, special interests.

We are already part of the United Nations, but we have yet to gain the global consciousness which can survive the tensions of international give and take. A compelling sense of purpose is a precondition to our acquiring the self-discipline to restrain shortsighted greed, unintelligent selfishness, and irrational aggressiveness which imperil social organization on a world scale. How otherwise can we have the morale to sustain sacrifices and launch out boldly into the great new enterprises demanded of us?

In other words, must we not become dedicated, consecrated, committed in ways which transcend "business as usual," "politics as usual," or "strikes as usual"? *The way of life called for at this moment of history is religious.* If religion, in the broadest sense, means giving the best we have to the highest we know, then certainly religious living is the greatest need of this hour. We need patience, poise, steadiness, reasonableness, firmness, courage, and unshakable faith. These are and always have been the fruits of creative, prophetic religion. This, it seems to me, is the first concrete situation that confronts us as we consider the place of religion in general education.

More than once before in the West has religion saved civilization. It would seem to be rather obvious also that to have such religion function effectively under the strain of the cold war, interrupted by flashes of hot war, citizens should be religiously educated. There ought to be some way for religion to be related to general education, so that every growing American may be possessed of a dynamic faith to work within the historic process for the spiritualization of individual living and the moral transformation of our society.

One of my old teachers used to love to quote, "When it is a duty to do a thing, it ought to be done. Simply because it is impossible is no excuse for refusing to do it. A large share of a man's best work in life consists of the accomplishment of the impossible when it must be done."

After a hundred years of increasing secularization of American life—and here I follow the definition of secular and secularization which Ernest Johnson has made familiar in religious thinking across the country through his books and articles and particularly in the report of the American Council on Education—it is a fact (of which some educators in teachers colleges seem insufficiently aware) that many persons who have in the past seen little value in religion are now beginning to turn to it in desperation. The recent nationwide rising tide of interest in religion is ample evidence that the majority of the American people would not knowingly or willingly accept the complete secularization of American education. This is another of those concrete situations which should be borne in mind as we search for solutions to the problem stated for us by Professor Johnson.

In the School of Education of New York University, we have assumed that there are at least four types of religious education which can be promoted without violation of the commonly accepted principle of separation of church and state. These are rather concrete.

1. There is the teaching as objectively as possible in the schools, by the school teachers, during regularly scheduled public school time, of the factual data of the Hebrew-Christian tradition. This would contain materials on which there are differences of opinion and interpretation, just as is true in the social studies.

This type of factual teaching might include the Bible, church history, history of religion, comparative religion. The teachers would not be indoctrinating in the interpretation of any particular religious group, but would be giving as facts what the positions of different groups are on the great events and documents and issues which are a part of the common religious heritage of the overwhelming majority of our people.

The decision of the Supreme Court in the Champaign case has no bearing whatever, I think, on this kind of teaching. In the curious and inaccurate use of the word, "secular," in the Supreme Court decision, this would be secular teaching of religious facts. We would prefer to call it non-sectarian instruction in religious facts. This should be done, may I repeat, in public school buildings, on school time, by school teachers, the same as we deal with every other controversial subject which is part of the general culture which everyone must know to be an educated person.

2. There is non-sectarian religious teaching of so-called secular subjects. Schools can do much more than they are doing on all subjects, particularly social studies and literature, with a view to securing awareness on the part of their pupils of the values which are highest in our democratic society; such as, for example, the intrinsic worth and essential dignity of human personality, the validity of the scientific method in determining the factors upon which judgments of value should be based, the cooperative nature of democratic experience, involving as it does the sharing of responsibilities and obligations as well as rights and privileges. Public schools should emphasize that the dynamic needed for living successfully in a democratic society is a creative faith in the validity of the religious principles on which our republic was founded.

I want to interrupt myself to say that I am not pleading for the introduction of the same brand of theism which was taught by the Founders in their schools at the beginning. In modern terms that would be sectarian. Humanism is a legitimate form of religion. There are those who are not theists as I am, and while I should prefer that others think as I do, it would seem improper for us to teach dogmatically in the schools the theistic position concerning religion, even if it was the belief of the Founding Fathers who have given us most of the great values on which our culture rests. What I am advocating here has no relation whatever to the propagation or indoctrination of anybody's dogma. However sacred they seem to many, or however time-honored, our particular doctrines should not be sponsored by the public schools. I want to make that very clear, in view of the fact that while I was a member of the committee which drafted the report of the International Council of Religious Education on "Religion and Public Education," published in February, 1949, I do not subscribe to the proposal set forth in that document.[1]

Most of all in public schools can you teach children and youth to make loyal commitments to the task of realizing the democratic dream through faithfulness, personal integrity, and social service. I think every school should, in relation to every subject it can, have two types of education. They are both religious but they deal with so-called secular subjects. The cue is valuational teaching aimed at discrimination in terms of value with a mind set toward choosing and making decisions in terms of the value which is higher. The other concerns outcome. Every bit of teaching, of everything whatsoever, should be pointed toward an outcome in social action, and if it does not eventuate in some appropriate form of social action, it is to that extent defective both educationally and religiously.

As a matter of strategy, it might be wiser not to use the word, "religion," about such a procedure at all. That would be all right with me, so long as we who are in the field of religion realize that we are talking about something religious.

Individual character, I believe, is realized through wholehearted participation in human relationships. This is an item of American faith which must be continually lifted up in every area of American education and celebrated suitably on national holidays.

That does not mean that you have chapel services in accord with the usage of the principal denomination, or that you have something which we recognize celebration to be another name for—worship. I think it would be a mistake to have in the public schools, promoted by public school faculties, forms of celebration which are recognized by men and women of other faiths as the liturgical form of worship of some particular group.

This work of developing character for democratic living is nonsectarian, although in a profound sense, because it deals with the conservation and increase of value, it is religious. That is why I have

[1] This report has appeared only in mimeographed form.

repeatedly called this second type of teaching "religious teaching of secular subjects." This, I repeat, should be done in public school buildings by trained public school people, on school time.

3. I am for a third form of religious education, which is frankly sectarian. And let me say that I accept the word, "sectarian," without flinching, because I know very well that my faith, from the standpoint of a good Jew or a good Roman Catholic, is sectarian. We often shrink from using the word about our own particular "broadminded" form of religion. We think that it is just religion; the other fellow is sectarian.

But I recognize the meaning of sectarian. Of course, the university does not teach a sectarian religion, but—and this is the third type of teaching I refer to—we do teach professional workers of various faiths and denominations, Roman Catholic, Jewish, and Protestant, how to propagate their own faith within their own institutions.

From the standpoint of the Supreme Court, any teaching of doctrines or tenets of any particular worshipping group is sectarian teaching. The fact that in circumstances similar to those obtaining in Champaign, Illinois, sectarian teaching is forbidden, does not at all relieve us of the necessity for greater emphasis upon better sectarian religious teaching where it can be legally done, for some of the most profound experiences which an individual may have are in public worship carried out corporately with likeminded believers who share a common history and tradition, common beliefs, and a common outreach toward the world. There is still need for the cultivation of admittedly sectarian religion, for the encouragement of sectarian religious education. In some schools of this type, students will learn that a personal religion in a historical orientation can still be relevant to everyday living at home, in school, on the playgrounds and streets, in every person-to-person and group relationship of our common life.

It is the duty of the university, the privately supported teachers college, or school of education, to train leaders for that task, as well as for the first two forms of religious education, which would be public.

Of course, the more obvious first step for religious groups is to make better use of the time that they now have in churches and synagogues and religious schools, on Saturdays and Sundays and during the summer.

4. But I would like to emphasize a fourth form of religious education of which certain aspects might be public and other aspects left to contacts of the sectarian groups, namely, religious teaching in the home. There is no law that prevents homes from being what they are and of right ought to be; that is, schools of religion. In this area, home and church and synagogue must work together. Churches and synagogues should, without delay, shift their major emphasis to helping parents learn how to use the everyday incidents of home life as the raw curricular material of religious nurture.

Colleges, universities, and seminaries should immediately introduce courses and curricula in parent education and religious family life, and a great many of them are doing it. I want to say that in that respect we shall have to have in teachers colleges and schools of education a very much better type of leadership education than we now have.

We have been teaching subjects—philosophy of education, educational psychology, educational sociology, tests and measurements in education, and many others—and the students, following the time-honored procedure, get the notes of the professor down in their notebooks and sometimes they do not pass through the minds of either in the process. Then after a time, we give the pupil a diploma and send him out into the wide, wide world to teach in public schools. We hope to heaven that the pupils will become teachers, but we have no assurance at all that an examination paper, or a term paper, or even a successful production of a doctor's dissertation, will enable them to handle boys and girls and their parents.

It is for that reason that we introduced three years ago first down in "The Village" [2] and then shifted to the Riverside Church, what we call a Workshop Combination, and we have modestly called it the best way to learn to teach religion. What we do is to take a series of procedures all of which are time-honored and proved and put them into one.

The educational workshop has been with us for a long time, and

[2] The neighborhood in which New York University's School of Education is located.

demonstration and observation classes have been used in teacher education even longer in the Laboratory School of Religious Education, started in Blairstown, New Jersey, by what was then the New Jersey Council of Religious Education, of which I had the honor to be general secretary. The practicum also was an old educational device whereby all instruction is based on the actual practice of an art, or science, and underlying principles are acquired inductively out of the solution of the problems which have arisen in a real situation.

The Workshop Combination—I am open for suggestions for a better name—is a combination of all of those well tried features— workshop, demonstration, observation school, laboratory school, and practicum seminar, plus a new feature which we shall be hearing about a great deal more in the future. That is, we assume that the homes are the major primary agencies of religious education. We follow the sixth chapter of Deuteronomy. I wish we had something like the "Shema" in Protestant Churches so that we would have to stand up and recite publicly, "And thou shalt teach them diligently unto thy children, and shalt talk of them when thou sittest in thy house."

Our assumption regarding the home in religious education means that the teachers must be taught how to visit homes and guide parents. We have a student go with a professionally trained, experienced teacher and see how he makes contact with the home. Then later, we have the student go out in company with the supervisor and the student does the talking to the parents, or listening, which is even better, for if you get the parents to open up, you can find much more by listening than by talking. The supervisor observes (without notebook or pencil) and talks it all over in the practicum afterwards—why, for instance, this suggestion misfired, and that one suddenly accelerated the process of producing *rapport* between the school and the home and led quickly to the solution of some problem in the life of the child.

I am very certain that although this is a terribly expensive procedure, it can be done more easily outside New York in more homogeneous cities than it can here. There will be need, perhaps, for a while, for endowed institutions that will bear the expense of doing it the best way they can. A lot of what is called teacher education in teachers colleges, both for public schools and for religious schools, is only a pious hope that it is leadership education.

But in this situation, we know, when we say to a school or a church, "I can recommend this man; I saw him do a piece of creative teaching out at"—let us say—"Floral Park, Long Island, and I know he can do it and that he can work with the parents," that at the end of four weeks' time these children show observable changes in their behavior.

Soldiers have a saying that "the battle is the payoff." In leadership education, the payoff is where the teacher sits down with a group of real persons, young people or children, or actually handles a parents' meeting. There is where we find out whether or not there has been leadership education.

What kind of students do we need to reach in terms of the total problem in privately supported schools of education? Two types, the ones that are going to be teachers in religious schools—Jewish, Catholic, and Protestant—and also those who are going to be teaching in public education, in secular schools, who need to understand the relevance of religion in the lives of boys and girls.

And we need to have two types of discipline, as well as two types of people, one intended for those who would like to become expert and well informed on religious education methodology, and one on the broader background subjects of religion.

While in schools of education religion is dealt with in departments of religious education, we really have to have courses in *religion,* as well as in religious education. I refer to such things as church history, philosophy of religion, history of religion, psychology of religion, sociology of religion, and comparative religion. I would like, if there were time, to indicate just why each of these is extremely important.

Then, too, we need courses which, while they are not usually considered technical courses in methodology in religious education, are related so closely to religious education that they must be included in the curriculum in a privately supported school of education. I refer to what we call now the clinical approach to personality prob-

lems in religious work. We used to call it solving personal problems. But these courses in counseling and guidance recognize the fact
that education is more reconstruction than instruction, also more
transformation than information, and more the receiving of power
than the mere receiving of facts. When you help people to remove
the obstacles and obstructions, whatever they may be, to creative,
joyous, affectionate, productive living, you are in the process of religious education.

Then, there are, of course, the definitely technical and professional
subjects—the principles of religious education, religious education of
children, religious education of adolescents, religious education of
adults, religion in the home, religion in public education, and numerous others. The ramification of these courses is very much wider
than you would think at first.

I would like to come back a moment to that first group of background courses, because that is where some of the best work can
be accomplished. It is always a thrilling experience for me to see each
year anew the response of students in our course entitled, "Religion
in World Culture," their expression when we calmly say, "Religion
is the mother not only of all the arts, but of all the sciences as
well," and then proceed in a couple of hours to prove it. The chances
are that in the social studies, the student has been using a textbook
which starts out with the spread of Christianity, for example, and
then tells of the invasion of the barbarians, next the Crusades, then
jumps several centuries into the heart of the Renaissance. Not a
word about how these barbarians became Christianized when they
came down into Rome, and then went back into the woods as missionaries and preceded the work of civilization in the places from
which their fathers and grandfathers came as soldiers. The cultural
outflowering of this influence, for example, is found in paintings
and in the Gothic cathedrals and in music, more out in the perimeter
than at Rome, the center from which the missionaries first came. That
development gets left out of the story all too often.

The publicly supported State or municipal school of education
labors under certain legal restrictions. There are things which it

should not do any more than elementary schools may properly do them. There are, to be sure, some homogeneous communities, where a State teachers college may teach religious content pretty much from the Protestant-Christian point of view with State funds. I do not believe that should be done in tax-supported institutions. I think that sort of education should be left to privately supported institutions.

A private institution may, through this Workshop Combination which I have described, have during the summer a Jewish unit with our Jewish students participating in Hebrew schools, and not a thing can be said against it. It would be comparable to our Workshop Combination in Riverside Church for Protestant-Christian students. Private teachers colleges can move out in some new directions experimentally, exploring channels which might not be so appropriate if done with taxpayers' money.

I would like to have a couple of million dollars for the establishment of a great child development and parent education center which would do something such as we have tried to do in the Workshop, dealing with every area related to a basic therapy—the preparation of parents; their relation to their surrounding culture; how to remove, by dealing with a parent's problem, some source of insecurity in a child who is learning and growing in the school; and the like.

Of course, I would also like to go much further in the exploration of the Workshop Combination. Institutions such as Teachers College at Columbia, New York University, Temple and Boston Universities, Harvard, Yale, and Pennsylvania, and many others, have a very special responsibility today for the entire task of improving both non-sectarian religious teaching in the schools and the frankly sectarian religious teaching in church and synagogue agencies.

The attitudes required at this time of statesmen as well as soldiers, of the citizens who follow, as well as those who lead, are developed only as we achieve on a large scale the integration of personality by a complete concentration upon inclusive purposes to which we can give ourselves with such devotion that we get out of it an experience of joy and thus have our creativity enhanced. In consequence, we become less aware of those things which divide us and disturb us and make us anxious and lonely. We can find the therapeutic value that is needed in these days in more wholehearted participation in this great social task of public education.

That, it seems to me, is the greatest challenge that comes to the privately supported teachers college in our time.

XI

RELIGION IN ELEMENTARY AND SECONDARY EDUCATION

BY

MATHEW P. GAFFNEY, LITT.D.

Superintendent, New Trier Township High School

I. The Issue

Francis Parker of Chicago once said that education consisted in presenting the right conditions for growth. Today most educators agree in general with this thesis, but what are the right conditions for growth?

Religion plays a major and fundamental part in man's life and, therefore, must be considered in studying these conditions. It is difficult to separate the spiritual child from the secular child because he is the same growing child. Such separation would be contrary to modern concepts of psychology and to our understanding of the nature of growth, and to everything we believe about the way in which a child matures. We realize that we are dealing with a whole boy, not with a family boy, or a school boy, or a church boy, or a community boy, or a movie-going boy.

From the historical point of view we find that religion has usually been present as a major reason for the establishment of schools. The Bill of Rights clearly recognizes the existence of religious ideas, while guaranteeing religious freedom.

Anson Phelps Stokes in his work on the church and the state has traced the long struggle in the development of a unique pattern of church-state relationships.[1] He says that historically our nation

[1] Anson Phelps Stokes, *Church and State in the United States,* Harper & Brothers, New York, 1950.

insisted upon and found ways of relating religion to education, but that lately we are witnessing a reversal of this trend. He warns that the failure to work out any satisfactory constitutional plan for providing a broad base for religious education for pupils of our public schools is one of the most serious weaknesses in the American system of religious freedom and church-state separation.

The United States, throughout its history, has been positive on the side of religion—not neutral. A study of the separation of church and state in this country indicates strongly that the whole intent was to avoid unfairness toward a minority religious view. It was anti-denominational, but it was not anti-religious. Rejecting a state religion with its attendant abuses was not rejecting religion as such.

Educators themselves have usually been concerned about ways to improve the teaching of moral and spiritual values. For example, the Educational Policies Commission of the National Education Association is at work at the present moment on such a study, the results of their deliberations to be published this spring [1951].[2]

There is little argument but that the school, along with the home, the church, and the community, shares a responsibility in developing moral and spiritual values. In some ways the school is in a favorable position, because the complex nature of our society means that we must at times think in terms of group values, and as the school deals with groups as well as with individuals, it is peculiarly well organized to inculcate the common moral principles which are essential in group living. Because the school also deals with children as individuals, it finds significance in the old rugged virtues of honesty, self-discipline, and integrity.

Of course there is always room for argument on what is a spiritual and what is an ethical value, but the dividing line is a thin one. Whatever the name, these values set standards, are motivating forces, and involve emotional responses. Moreover, these emotions develop from many sources. They may come from contemplation of nature, from the arts—literature, painting, music, or drama—but from whatever source they spring, their inception, their growth, and their expression become a major concern of all good schools.

[2] Cf. pp. 200 f.

It seems obvious, therefore, that a first responsibility of all schools is to create such an atmosphere that spiritual values can arise and that such emotional responses can be called forth. The objectives of the school as evidenced by the life of the school must be favorable to the development of spiritual values. Writers agree generally that a study of the child and his educational needs and the laws governing his growth and development make it clear that the school cannot ignore his spiritual growth, along with his physical, mental, social, and emotional growth.

When we turn from the child himself to the world in which he lives at the present time and in which he is going to live, what do we see? At the present moment we see a world of violence, of conflicting ideologies, of changing values in once stable institutions. In the home we often find a disintegration of family life and breakdown of family authority. With increased divorce has come lowering of family standards and insecurity for the child.

Whatever the present position of the church may be, it is surely a very different position from that held by the church of fifty years ago in the rural districts where most of the people of a half century ago lived. Moreover, the shift from rural to urban populations has brought dislocations with loss of intimacy and corresponding loss of personal responsibility. This has been emphasized by the change in the relation of man to his work. The shoemaker finished an entire shoe and had a feeling of pride in accomplishment, but the piece worker lacks this satisfaction, and the loss of reality and responsibility is increased.

Another factor resulting in loss of a feeling of personal responsibility is the hugeness and complexity of business, government, and large city systems. I remember a small village where my uncle owned a general store, and because that gave him an important position in the life of the village he and his wife felt great personal and civic responsibility and were people of strong influence for good. It would be hard to think of the manager of the average chain store sharing a similar position in the community or feeling the same sense of responsibility.

Along with the growing complexity of big business has gone

the growing complexity of big government with its bureaucracies and its unfortunate distance from the individual. This again tends to lessen the individual's feeling of responsibility. The same is seen in the tremendous school systems of our great cities, the huge State universities, and all great organizations where the individual gets lost in the system.

With the impersonality of the great machine inevitably comes a lessening of the feeling of personal importance and personal responsibility. To add to this, present-day psychiatry—or would it be fairer to say a false interpretation of psychiatry—tends to lessen the feeling of the person's responsibility for his own acts. In the school with which I am connected, I have more than a few times had boys and girls when faced with a misdemeanor, explain glibly, "That is all right because my psychiatrist says we all have certain drives and this is the way I work out this drive. It is perfectly natural." Right and wrong, the effect on others or on oneself, does not seem to enter into the problem, just an understanding of nature's drives. Again, this breaks down any feeling of personal responsibility.

One could develop at length the picture of the increasing cheapness and vulgarity of certain aspects of present-day living. Today's child is surrounded with such influences as the movie, the radio, television, cheap newspapers, the so-called funnies, the cheap pulp magazines, the all-out effort to advertise sex, alcohol, and tobacco. Thirty years ago it was common in areas where I lived for dinner parties to be held without having cocktails served; then there was the period of *a* cocktail; now we live in the era of rounds of cocktails. As recently as twenty-five years ago, away from the big cities, women did not smoke in public. Today, mothers coming to school on errands often go through our corridors without putting out their cigarettes, and if they come in my office, they often light up without a "by your leave." Since I have been in New York on this trip, I saw an item in the morning paper stating that more narcotic hospitals are being urged for youth, because of the tremendous growth in the use of narcotics by adolescents.

As a result of two world wars, we have had great social disasters, the resurgence of barbarisms, the callousness of war carried into civilian life, again greatly lessening personal responsibility, because when you hand yourself over to Uncle Sam the plans are made for you and you fit into them.

A phase of our times is the increased emphasis on sex in advertising, in movies, and in plays. If you were a high school principal responsible for approving the selection of school plays, you would be conscious of how few plays there are that are suitable for the adolescent to produce, study, and act.

If I have given a recognizable picture of the world our children live in, even though I have purposely shown only the dark side of the picture, is it not obvious that young people must be helped to develop inner moral restraints sufficiently powerful to combat impulses toward brutality and to guide them toward high goals? Above all, is it not of first importance to create situations that require the assumption of personal responsibility?

The new position of world leadership that we as Americans hold —do we have the spiritual force and maturity to make it real leadership? If I have painted a gloomy picture, let me change my brush. I do not feel gloomy about the future. Perhaps no nation ever had the opportunity for good that we have right now. Our children have a unique world opportunity, but are they going to be able to take advantage of it? Are they going to live up to this challenge and what are we as schools doing to help?

Lastly, we Americans are not homogeneous. Our schools deal with children of many races, many cultural backgrounds, many social and economic backgrounds, many religions. What does this mean for education? Are there common spiritual values, common ideals, common standards, common points of view, sympathies, and understandings, that it becomes the duty of the school to clarify?

The answer is obviously, "Yes," if in spite of our differences we are to be a united people, and a people worthy of our great heritage.

II. The Problem

There will be little disagreement so far. Parents want good children, the churches are against sin, and the schools want to do their duty. Then why has this subject been so much to the fore in recent years, and why are we considering it at present?

Of course certain recent court decisions have focused attention on the problem, but I believe they are results rather than causes. The real reason is the growing tension and suspicion between various religious groups and the hesitancy of schoolmen to be drawn into situations that cannot be controlled. The complete difference in belief about such things as religious authority and the source of religious sanctions makes it impossible for the Protestant to understand the Roman Catholic, or the Roman Catholic to understand the Christian Scientist in matters of religion. A personal experience that I had a few years ago points up the difficulty.

I had hoped that in our relatively homogeneous and highly civic-minded community it would be possible to get agreement from our churches on a common plan of action. It was hoped that the problem could be worked out in cooperation with the churches, and we invited every church in our township to send a representative to a committee which would work on the problem of religious education in our school. I believe all the churches had representatives and in most cases it was the minister, priest, or rabbi. These people met at intervals for a year and a half and for me it was a disillusioning experience. Three camps emerged.

One camp was for religious education on school time and in the school building, but only if taught by their official spiritual leaders and completely denominational in character. This group held that there is no such thing as religious education unless it is dogmatic and denominational in character. They wished the children to be separated by denominations and each group taught according to its beliefs.

A second camp wanted no denominational teaching. These people wanted a course for all children that would study the growth and development of the idea of religion, that would help children appreciate the different contributions of the Jew, the Roman Catholic, the Protestant, the Bahaist, and the Christian Scientist. The course would deal with the history of religion and with comparative religion, with the spiritual forces back of all religions, but would avoid any denominational teaching as such. Such a course they hoped would be taught not by priests, rabbis, or ministers, but by the teachers of the public high school.

In the argument one interesting point came to light that showed the complete conflict of ideas. A young minister remarked, "I think we should create a course that will help these young people to decide for themselves what to believe." Immediately members of the other camp jumped in with, "No! No! We shall *tell* them what to believe."

The third camp wanted nothing of either of the above approaches. They said in so many words, "We prefer to have the school leave the matter of religion entirely alone. We shall handle religious education in our own churches as our particular responsibility." Their attitude toward the other two groups was, "A plague on both your houses."

In the year and a half that these good people met, I doubt that there was a deviation from their original positions. The only agreement they reached was that no agreement seemed possible.

I quote this experience because I think it is of more than local significance. I have talked with principals and superintendents from many states and I believe this is a common experience, and I am perfectly aware of a few places where other things have been tried and seemingly with some success. However, when we as schoolmen tangle with the vested interests and sincere convictions of the various denominations, we are in deep water.

As far as the legal aspects are concerned, I personally believe that eventually recent decisions may be reversed, and legal restrictions removed, but I do not think these are the fundamental problems. The problem comes from the religious groups themselves.

In spite, therefore, of the urgent need for moral and spiritual training in public schools, it is blocked—there is an impasse. Does this mean we must accept a defeatist attitude and do nothing? Not at all! It may mean a different and new direction which at first may not satisfy those who for years have interpreted religious education in certain definite ways. It may demand a greater insight and a greatly expanded conception of what is involved in religious education, and a willingness to concede that those things which are denominational in character belong in the churches and not in the schools. It will, of course, lay itself open to the accusation that "such and such" is not religion but ethics, that it is avoidance of the issue, that it is compromise, but I am convinced that such accusations will be based on a lack of understanding of the basic drives in human behavior and of the sources of religious strength.

Moreover, until such time as the schools have done well those things that they can do without running into opposition with the sincerely held beliefs of certain religious groups, I wonder if they should not put their efforts into improving those aspects of their curriculum and activities on which agreement can be reached.

III. Outcomes or Solutions

My position will be that there are certain ideas and practices basic to spiritual and moral growth, to religious education if you will, which the schools are particularly well fitted to meet.

The Christian and Jewish faiths are founded on belief in the worth of the individual as an individual as opposed to the totalitarian concept of the individual as a tool of the state. The school's first duty, therefore, is through the administration, the organization, the teaching, the guidance, through all the learning and living that takes place in the school to emphasize and respect the worth of each individual, and to inculcate such respect in all boys and girls. The school must give every child an opportunity to grow to his full physical, mental, moral, emotional, and spiritual stature, to develop his self-respect and integrity.

What are some of the ways by which this can be done? Take the curriculum first. There has been a growth in recent years of a procedure called pupil-planning. In brief, all this means is that there are certain areas in education where a pupil can make his own decisions and lay out plans for his own work. He can realize that not every idea is taken on authority, but that there are intellectual processes one can chart for himself.

Recently I heard the provost of a great educational institution discussing the need for this very ability. He said that even on the graduate level his students were often very unhappy if they could not find authority for every idea, whereas, intellectual maturity consists in realizing that certain responsibilities we must assume for ourselves. The very curriculum, therefore, can be used in building up for an individual a concept of his responsibility, his importance, and his worth.

In the school with which I am connected, when I face a class of 600 ninth graders, I know that I am facing youngsters who have reading abilities from fourth grade level to adult as shown by standard tests. I know that if we put these extremes together, give them the same materials and treat them in the same way, we are completely disregarding their worth as individuals. The child who cannot read the material will decide he is a hopeless failure, will probably become a disciplinary problem and will soon drop out of school.

At a recent meeting of the National Secondary School Principals' Association a speaker reported that sixty-six per cent of the children in the country as a whole who entered kindergarten never finished the twelfth grade. Whether the figure is exact or not, the picture is shocking, and it emphasizes the point that no matter how good the curriculum may be, it is no good for the children who drop out and get no part of it.

There is a certain industrial city in Illinois where this situation came to light in a recent study. The administration had been conscious of many drop-outs, but until a careful study was made last year they had not sensed that they were losing nearly half of all students who entered the ninth grade before graduation in the twelfth. They made a definite effort to find the reason and sent questionnaires to hundreds of young men and women who had dropped from school during the past ten years. Two main reasons came immediately to light. The first reason was, "We didn't feel we were getting anything worthwhile for us." These drop-outs tended to come from the lower economic and social groups, and tended to be in lower ability groups as shown by standard tests.

The second reason given was, "It cost too much money. Because we were in school we were not income earners, in the first place. Then everything took money—football games, basketball, school parties, dances, clubs, and the like. If we decided to take home economics or industrial arts instead of Latin, the fees were prohibitive. The very things we needed and could do always cost more. Because of the combination of poor grades, failures, constant need for money, we finally gave up and left school."

This particular city went to work to meet its problem. New courses were developed to meet the needs of slow learners. The school board eliminated fees and made school activities available to all students. Even in six months there was a marked increase in the holding power of that particular school.

In our school in the ninth grade we have as many as six sections in English alone, and they all receive credit for freshman English. Some of them are practically classes in reading, whereas others are doing a quality of work amazingly high. It is possible for a student to succeed on his own level and, therefore, develop a feeling of his own worth as an individual. Year after year it is thrilling to see that high officers in school activities, leaders in all branches, leaders in plays and operas and athletics, and student council can be young people who started very low in the academic scale, but who possess unusual abilities of other kinds. In fact, students who start the ninth grade in very special classes often make remarkable academic adjustment in later years. To be a very poor student in the ninth grade may be due to limited mental capacity, but it may also be due to emotional blocks, to physical reasons, to poor preparation, to language difficulties, or to many other factors. Twenty years ago when we presented to our board of education the idea of special classes for retarded students, we really believed that these pupils were definitely limited mentally. We predicted that we could keep them about two years and then they would reach the limit of their educability and they would drop out. That just did not happen. Many of them made excellent adjustments to normal high school classes.

I have one illustration of a boy who entered our ninth grade as a very retarded case, who graduated from high school, graduated from college, and is now an admissions officer in a large university.

Academically, we thought he was low mentally and tests at that time indicated it, but it proved not to be so.

Some years ago a parent, a psychiatrist, and an elementary school head made an appointment with me. They had a very strange request. The son of the parent involved had just failed the seventh grade for the second time. There were evidences in his case that he was an unusually bright boy, but extremely maladjusted in many ways. The people working with him felt that if he repeated the seventh grade a third time, he would fail again, because he felt he was "getting even" with a hostile world by doing nothing that he was supposed to. They felt that he would have the same emotional reaction in the eighth grade in the same school and same environment, but that if he could be moved to the freshman year of high school with a completely clean slate, he might adjust and succeed. We accepted the recommendation and the challenge and allowed this boy to enter the ninth grade. He not only passed every subject, but continued for four years in high school with never a failure.

I am not sure what moral I am trying to draw from that except that a feeling of individual worth can be developed in school and is basic to the whole question of moral and spiritual values.

To move to the field of student activities, these values can be made vital. Our particular student council runs successfully student-supervised study halls that take care of over half the students in school. To be able to take care of yourself in an honor study hall is considered a mark of distinction. Our council also manages the lunch hall, studies problems of recreation, develops an honor system, and keeps interest in it alive, and has produced a code of ethics for New Trier students.

An example of their constructive work is the Halloween party. Years ago there were some unfortunate incidents in our community on Halloween. The council decided to furnish recreation on that night, and it has developed into one of the big affairs of the year. This past fall at least 2,000 boys and girls participated in activities which used the auditorium, dining hall, library, swimming pool, all gyms, and field house. The party is so large that we get faculty members and parents to assist, but all planning and organization are done by students. Our students through their New Trier Girls Club and Tri Ship Boys Club are very active in the field of service, and learn that they have responsibility not only for themselves, but for other people and for institutions. They raise money to build up scholarships in college for those who need such help, they form groups to handle our complicated traffic situation, to usher at all school events and all community events that use the school building, to meet people entering the school and to get them whatever information is needed, to act as door guards during lunch hours, to act as library aides, service club girls, senior helpers in freshman adviser rooms and many other capacities.

The students have not stopped at the service level, however. They have raised the activities to a higher level by studying the purpose of such activities and the place they hold in an educational program. Years ago our faculty worked out a philosophy and a copy of this got into the hands of a student. The next thing we knew our council was working on a philosophy for the student council. They studied this for a year and produced a statement which has been their guiding philosophy ever since and which gives meaning to their activities. Soon after this our New Trier Tri Ship Boys Club to which every boy automatically belongs became interested in the matter of citizenship and produced a document attempting to explain what is involved in being a good citizen in a public school, what kinds of citizens there are, and how to change from a negative to a positive or contributing citizen.

The students have also worked on an honor system for examinations and have learned that one must work at it constantly, that interest and participation must be stimulated anew every semester. They have created a code of ethics and every year they try new ways to get this accepted by every boy and girl.

All activity of this type involves cooperation, involves an acceptance of personal responsibility, and involves control. Students learn that one has desires of one's own which one controls in order to create a better situation for other people and in so doing one develops moral responsibility and devotion to truth.

When students can tackle important problems they are capable of clear and critical thinking. I have just had an example of that. For many years in our school we have had a most exciting spring election to an honor society and in recent years excitement was built up to hysterical proportions. When it was proposed to do away with this election there was a storm of protest, and so we asked the student council to take a year to study the matter. After a year of study the student recommendations are much more drastic than faculty or parent recommendations.

In such ways students develop a devotion to truth and clear thinking, a desire for constructive action, a respect for the achievement of each one on his own level. This includes a respect for excellence for those capable of excellence. This involves a respect for the religious opinions of others. Individual integrity and personal devotion become involved. If schools can develop strongly the feeling of the worth of the individual, the feeling of each one's personal responsibility and his group responsibility, and the view that part of one's life should be devoted to the welfare of others and to the sympathetic understanding of others, then the schools are making a great contribution to the moral and spiritual life of boys and girls.

Is there any better foundation that the schools can build?

On this foundation each church can work to rear its own edifice to make sure that the City of God is present in the heart of man.

XII

SUMMARY AND CONCLUSIONS [1]

BY

F. ERNEST JOHNSON

Any attempt at a summary of a number of thoughtful addresses must be highly selective, but when the subject is controversial the "summarizing" must have implicit in it some argument or direction of thought. For the present purpose I go back for guidance to the statement of the main problem confronting us with which we began our exploration: "How can public education, in accord with its function of putting each generation in possession of its full cultural heritage, do justice to the religious phase of that heritage without doing violence to religious liberty as constitutionally safeguarded in the First Amendment to the American Constitution and in similar provisions in the constitutions of the several States?" I am impressed with the extent to which the several speakers have kept their eyes on this goal.

To be sure, the scope of the series has been broader than that single question suggests, for there has been much discussion of non-public education. But this has served to illumine the purposes of general education which public and non-public schools have in common, and so to define more clearly the problem of finding the place of religion in public education. It was instructive, indeed, to be told how the "acids of modernity" have eaten into the traditions of a once explicitly Christian institution.

We have been repeatedly reminded that the educative process has

[1] As noted in the Foreword, this address has been revised and extended to take account of significant developments between the termination of the course and the time of going to press.

a unitary quality which makes a dualism of the secular and the religious unrealistic. In particular, our glimpses of higher education have shown that it is quite impossible to exclude religious subject matter from an educational program without warping it. We have had brought to our attention tax-supported institutions of higher learning in which the claims of religion are frankly recognized. I think the weight of the testimony we have heard indicates that the doctrine seemingly laid down by the United States Supreme Court in the Everson and McCollum cases, calling for absolute separation of the spheres of government and religion, is remote from the realities of the educational situation.

This view of the matter has now been given impressive support in the decision of the Supreme Court, handed down on April 28, 1952, confirming the constitutionality of the released-time plan of weekday religious education operating in New York City. The case (*Zorach v. Clauson, et al.*) is relevant to this discussion chiefly because the majority of the Court took a very different view of the meaning of the First and Fourteenth Amendments with respect to separation of church and state, from that set forth in the Everson and McCollum cases. Indeed, the extremely sharp dissents of three members of the Court serve to emphasize the about-face of our highest tribunal on this controversial issue. The contrast between the Zorach doctrine and the Everson-McCollum doctrine stands out in the following passages from the ruling opinion in the Zorach case:

There is much talk of the separation of Church and State in the history of the Bill of Rights and in the decisions clustering around the First Amendment. . . . There cannot be the slightest doubt that the First Amendment reflects the philosophy that Church and State should be separated. And so far as interference with the "free exercise" of religion and an "establishment" of religion are concerned, the separation must be complete and unequivocal. The First Amendment within the scope of its coverage permits no exception; the prohibition is absolute. The First Amendment, however, does not say that in every and all respects there shall be a separation of Church and State. Rather, it studiously defines the manner, the specific ways, in which there shall be no concert or union or dependency one on the other. That is the common sense of the matter. Otherwise the state and religion would be aliens to each other—hostile, suspicious, and even unfriendly. Churches could not be required to pay even property taxes. Municipalities would not be permitted to render police or fire protection to religious groups. Policemen who helped parishioners into their places of worship would violate the Constitution. Prayers in our legislative halls; the appeals to the Almighty in the messages of the Chief Executive; the proclamations making Thanksgiving Day a holiday; "so help me God" in our courtroom oaths —these and all other references to the Almighty that run through our laws, our public rituals, our ceremonies would be flouting the First Amendment. A fastidious atheist or agnostic could even object to the supplication with which the Court opens each session: "God save the United States and this Honorable Court."

We would have to press the concept of separation of Church and State to these extremes to condemn the present law on constitutional grounds. The nullification of this law would have wide and profound effects. A Catholic student applies to his teacher for permission to leave the school during hours on a Holy Day of Obligation to attend a mass. A Jewish student asks his teacher for permission to be excused for Yom Kippur. A Protestant wants the afternoon off for a family baptismal ceremony. In each case the teacher requires parental consent in writing. In each case the teacher, in order to make sure the student is not a truant, goes further and requires a report from the priest, the rabbi, or the minister. The teacher in other words cooperates in a religious program to the extent of making it possible for her students to participate in it. Whether she does it occasionally for a few students, regularly for one, or pursuant to a systematized program designed to further the religious needs of all the students does not alter the character of the act. . . .

When the State encourages religious instruction or cooperates with religious authorities by adjusting the schedule of public events to sectarian needs, it follows the best of our traditions. For it then respects the religious nature of our people and accommodates the public service to their spiritual needs. To hold that it may not would be to find in the Constitution a requirement that the government show a callous indifference to religious groups. That would be preferring those who believe in no religion over those who do believe. Government may not finance religious groups nor undertake religious instruction nor blend secular and sectarian education nor use secular institutions to force one or some religion on any person. But we find no constitutional requirement which makes it necessary for government to be hostile to religion and to throw its weight against efforts to widen the effective scope of religious influence. The government must be neutral when it comes to competition between sects. It may not thrust any sect on any person. It may not make a religious observance compulsory. It may not coerce anyone to attend church, to observe a religious holiday, or to take religious instruction. But it can close its doors or suspend its operations as to those who want to repair to their religious sanctuary for worship or instruction. No more than that is undertaken here.

The words, "encourages" and "cooperates," in the above passages are especially significant since it has been generally assumed that what they connote was definitely precluded in the McCollum case.

There is much in these words for lawyers to debate and they may be counted on to do so. The fact that the Court declared, "We follow the McCollum case," while at the same time repudiating the interpretation of the Constitution that has been generally found in that case, is very confusing to the lay mind. But the Zorach doctrine furnishes a new basis for consideration of the legal aspects of the problem dealt with in this series of addresses.

We should not lose sight of the Court's explicit statement that government may not "undertake religious instruction nor blend secular and sectarian education nor use secular institutions to force one or some religion on any person." This seems to exclude religious indoctrination of any type from the curriculum of the tax-supported schools. Does it also exclude the objective study of religious subject matter as it appears in the various disciplines—history, literature, art, and so on? The latter is what the Educational Policies Commission proposes in its widely discussed report, *Moral and Spiritual Values in the Public Schools*. No sure answer can be given to this question, but there is good reason to believe that non-indoctrinational study of religion as a part of the culture will not fall under the ban.

Not only is religious subject matter necessarily included in a culturally adequate educational program, but some kind of cooperative relationship between church and school seems to be inevitable, unless we are violently to disrupt well established patterns of American community life. I confess to some change in my own thought on this point. It appears that the relationship between church and school in many American communities is something deeper—though largely intangible—than we who live in large cosmopolitan cities have realized.

I wish to make myself quite clear on this question, which is at best involved and difficult. It has all along seemed to me vitally important to maintain the separation between the church and the secular state in public education. My colleague, Professor R. Freeman Butts, has argued strongly against the theory that the relationship between the church and the state in American education is one of "cooperation" rather than separation.[2] The argument has much cogency, for cooperation is a word with a very broad coverage of possibilities, and its free use tends toward obliteration of functional distinctions. I am, to be sure, quite as convinced as ever that it is idle, even reactionary, to seek in the writings of the Founding Fathers any adequate prescription for present practice. Most of us would never think of looking to them as final authority in any other sphere. Moreover, the record of the Constitutional debates is to my mind not nearly so clear and conclusive as many people find it. But the Founders' concern that the state should not be a party to any effort to spread religious beliefs about which honest men differ, has for me an authentic quality undiminished by the passing of time.

Furthermore, we were told from this platform in memorable words how great a stake a minority group, itself very responsive to the claims of religious education, has in the constitutional safeguards against application of religious pressures by sheer force of numbers. Surely we have been late in recognizing the permanent and inevitable hazard to personal liberty that is implicit in majority rule. And in no sphere is the intrusion of state power more disastrous than in that of religion.

Nevertheless, with due regard for all these considerations, in the light of these addresses and of recent events I find myself more impressed than ever before with the difficulty of making an "absolute" out of the separation between church and state with respect to education. A large proportion of the people who send their children to

2 R. Freeman Butts, *The American Tradition in Religion and Education*, The Beacon Press, New York, 1950.

school also send them to church, in both cases for the purpose of being educated. The school teachers and administrators are important elements in lay church leadership. The currents of religious and secular thought and interest cannot, even in a secular society, be kept isolated. For those members of the community, usually a substantial majority, who are related both to school and to church the sanctions of religion are too highly revered to admit of their being ignored by the school even though they may not be explicitly invoked. And in many communities—let us face it—religion is such a pervasive influence that to eliminate all religious observances from school assemblies would be a major operation. The fact that the pressure for recognition of religion in the schools comes often from people who give it scant recognition in their business and professional lives, grievous though this is, does not make the problem less serious. Certainly it would be very difficult to make operationally practicable the doctrine apparently laid down in the McCollum case concerning the complete elimination of religious features from the school program. The federal courts are not equipped to function as school boards in managing the program of public education. This is one of the areas in which the maintenance of a principle requires a continual, experimental drawing and redrawing of lines. The setting up of absolute requirements is both impracticable and undesirable.

This problem, however, loses nothing of its urgency through being too complex to admit of solution by formula. Although I am increasingly skeptical of any attempt, administrative, legislative or judicial, to impose one pattern on our schools, I remain strongly opposed to any policy which makes the tax-supported schools responsible for inculcating religious beliefs. To this subject we shall return later.

As this series proceeded, a need has appeared for a clearer understanding of what we mean by religion. The confusion we noted at the outset over the meaning of religion has not, it seems to me, been wholly cleared up. There is still a tendency, in such discussions as we have had here, to define religion in two very different ways. On the one hand, we treat it as consisting in beliefs and observances which are distinct, definite, and in practice often divisive; on the other hand, we speak of it as a common spiritual and ethical outlook that is expressed in the Golden Rule. In the one case it is considered sectarian, and therefore to be guarded against; in the other case it is universal and therefore belongs in every school, every day!

In stating our problem at the beginning of the course I alluded to this confusion in a way that was perhaps not wholly fair in its implication. After all, it is inherent in the subject and is not due to mere perversity in argument. Let us consider, for example, the definition of religion given in a recently published book by one of the most eminent representatives of what is sometimes called the Dewey school of educational philosophy. Professor William H. Kilpatrick proposes to define religion, for practical purposes, as "the spirit with which one holds one's supreme value—the value in terms of which one values all else—plus the outworking of this attitude appropriately in life." [3] Now this seems to me a quite acceptable psychological definition of a religious attitude—the religious "spirit." I would say without reservation that no study of religion that does not take account of this aspect of it can be adequate.

At the same time, from a philosophical viewpoint the study of religion must include the various ways in which men have conceived this ultimate value "in terms of which one values all else." And from a sociological point of view the study of religion includes the various institutions in which and through which men have pursued their religious quest. To stop with the individual phase of religious experience, neglecting its corporate, institutional expression, would be like studying politics without reference to political parties, or economics without looking at corporations, banks, and labor unions. Religion is overwhelmingly social—something men corporately *do*. When so understood, its place in general education would seem to need no argument. And the reason why anything in the nature of doctrinal instruction in religion is such a grievous problem for public education is precisely the same as the reason why partisan political and economic indoctrination has to be avoided in the schools. It is because equally intelligent and equally sincere people differ on these questions.

[3] William H. Kilpatrick, *Philosophy of Education,* The Macmillan Company, New York, 1951, p. 157.

I think the presentations we have had here of Protestant, Catholic, and Jewish positions ought to make it clear that the effort to reduce them all to a common denominator can never succeed. Moreover, we have had fresh evidence that the trouble experienced by Horace Mann over a hundred years ago may still attend any effort to reach agreement on religious essentials. We have listened to an account of one school superintendent's frustrating experience in connection with such an effort. The things we do agree about are, to be sure, part and parcel of our religious systems, but these agreements concern *moral,* or *spiritual,* assumptions and aims, many of which are quite as tenaciously held by many people who disclaim religious faith entirely as by those who make the sincerest religious profession. It cannot be too strongly emphasized that the case for inclusion of religious subject matter in the study program of the schools is not strengthened by contending that only "believers" can be good citizens and good democrats. Evidence to the contrary is abundant. There is no "core" of religious faith that can be inculcated in our public schools which a substantial part of the community may not reasonably regard as sectarian. The one point upon which it seems reasonable to hope for agreement about religion in the context of the present discussion is this, that religion has been and is too important a factor in the life of man to be ignored in general education.

Let us make this matter concrete and timely by frankly examining the policy statement issued in November, 1951, by the Board of Regents of the State of New York concerning the introduction of a prayer in the school program and the deliberate cultivation of a religious faith as part of the school's responsibility. The suggested prayer reads as follows: "Almighty God, we acknowledge our dependence upon Thee, and we beg Thy blessing upon us, our parents,. our teachers, and our country." The Board proposes "specific programs stressing the moral and spiritual heritage which is America's." The children are to be "constantly confronted with the basic truth of their existence"; all their studies are thus to be "brought into focus and accord"; each of them will be "properly prepared to follow the faith of his or her father," as expounded by their respective religious leaders; and so "the school will fulfil its high function of supplementing the training of the home, ever intensifying in the child that love for God, for parents and for home, which is the mark of true character training and the sure guaranty of a country's welfare." I am disposed to make two quite distinct comments about these proposals.

First, there is the matter of the prayer. If we are to take seriously the democratic control of our schools, and the intimate relation that should exist between them and the community, I think an attempt to exclude all religious symbolism, *when it is an authentic expression of the mood of the community as a whole,* is artificial and forced. And I do not see how a reverent act of the kind proposed as a part of the school ritual, which is understood to commit none but those who freely join in it, and in the absence of pressure of any kind, will do violence to the sensibilities of any intelligent and serious-minded person when its significance is understood. A reverent person reveres the faiths of his fellows. I should like to see prevail a public educational policy that would leave a school board, as representative of a community, free to introduce some sort of religious symbolism, not as a concession to outside pressures, but as a carefully considered policy. We must not forget the last part of the religious clause of the First Amendment. Government is restrained not only from any act tending toward an establishment of religion, but from "prohibiting the free exercise thereof." If and where a community feels so strongly about religion in relation to the education of its children that it insists on some token of religious faith within the school, what we are dealing with is an elemental demand for religious liberty. Anticipating the discussion of secularism to which we shall turn presently, let me say that failure to take account of liberty as a group, and not exclusively an individual, right, is at the root of much of our difficulty in church-state relations.

That this way of putting the matter is controversial I am well aware. Indeed, my concern is not so much to win acceptance for the conclusions I am venturing to put forward as to have the problem recognized as something that cannot be shrugged off, or settled by glib repetition of a legal formula.

It is to be hoped, however, that any attempt to introduce a corporate prayer in a school assembly will be subject to a voluntary choice by the community which the school represents. Is it not fair also to require that the administrators and teachers involved accept responsibility for guarding pupils from pressure, direct or indirect, to participate in an act of worship?

But the policy statement of the New York Board of Regents lends itself, in part, to an interpretation that seems to cut across the distinction we have tried to make between the role of public education and that of religious education in a non-public school. Taken as a whole, it seems to me the papers in this series do not warrant the assumption by tax-supported schools of responsibility for intensive religious education. The reason for the restriction now held to be implicit in the First Amendment is not merely the danger of sectarian strife, but that of establishing a kind of dogmatic instruction which in the nature of the case could not have the full and honest sanction of more than a part of the community. Also, making the public school responsible for inculcating religious beliefs and fostering religious attitudes would mean introducing a religious test for school teachers—one that would exclude a substantial number of conscientious persons whose religious views are not clear enough to warrant their acceptance of such a responsibility. By the same token, would it not inevitably put a premium on duplicity or superficiality on the part of prospective teachers who might too lightly assume an obligation they are unprepared to discharge?

In the course of this series of addresses we have been confronted by a need for clarifying another concept, namely, that of secularism. It was discussed for us at some length as related to publicly supported higher education in a way that illustrated its wide ramifications. But differences of opinion were apparent.

In general, it has not seemed to me necessary in this review to refer to individual participants in the series by name. An exception should be made in the case of the one contribution in which a major assumption that underlies the analysis presented at the outset was challenged. Dr. Thayer's argument concerning the significance of secularism was ably presented and calls for most careful and sym-

method—which Dr. Thayer identifies with secularism—of dealing with controversy in non-religious matters—politics, economics, and the like. For these *are* dealt with in our schools as serious and persistent human concerns, except where reactionary influences will not allow it. Educators do not argue that because they belong in the secular sphere they have no place in the schools.

The authentic public method of handling controversial issues in the schools is that which Dr. Thayer so well describes. To repeat, it is of the essence of secularism, as I understand it, to exclude religious subject matter from the educational program on the ground that it is irrelevant—that it does not have a place in general education. The contention that religion is too hot to handle, is the identical objection that reactionary critics of the schools have made to the introduction of controversial social problems in the curriculum. And some of the stoutest contenders for their introduction are found in the ranks of those who say of religion, "Why bring that in?"

Nothing is more characteristic of the secularist viewpoint than the argument that religion must be excluded whenever it appears divisive. Political and economic questions are divisive, too. Those courageous educators and lay educational leaders who have fought reaction time after time in the battle over the social studies know very well that these studies are divisive, but they also believe they are *important* and an integral part of general education. When people argue that religious subject matter must not be studied under public school auspices, they are usually, I think, recording a judgment that, unlike politics and economics, religion is quite "expendable" in general education.

We have had illuminating discussions in this country at the highest judicial level of the validity of the requirement that all school pupils salute the flag. When the Supreme Court reversed itself in this matter and decided against compulsion, many of us thought the decision a wise and liberating one. But has any one suggested that because a few families objected to the ceremony on religious grounds the school should abandon it? When the exercise of a fundamental corporate freedom is wholly inhibited on the ground of individual dissent, the whole matter is out of focus. What is indi-

pathetic study. Its importance in this context lies not so
his conclusions concerning the actual place of religion in
curriculum, as in the philosophic position he ably represen

Dr. Thayer made a notable attempt to define the wor
larism": it "represents an effort to carve out areas of commo
ment and common action as between people whose interests
and who disagree vigorously in matters they consider fundar
It follows that "secular education is an education dedicated
development of disciplined ways of thinking and living t
designed to further a free communication between people of
background and diverse convictions who live of necessity in a
sensitive and interdependent world. It is an education that c
trates upon methods of procedure appropriate to controversial
such as politics, social relations, economic life, as well as reli
methods of procedure that insure a fair hearing for all inter
parties and grind the ax for none." Now it seems to me that
Thayer has here described not what is "secularist" but wha
public. What is public, and hence inclusive, must be under se
direction in order to be non-sectarian. But *secularism* is a t
with a history and I think it must be defined in relation to its hist
It is widely used to denote, not the secular areas of life, but a v
of living and thinking that makes the secular self-sufficient a
renders religion irrelevant. If secularism connoted nothing but t
secular areas of life, there would be no argument over it. Once th
system of public education became in scope and design a preparatio
for *living,* any area of human concern arbitrarily excluded from
was automatically relegated to a position of inferior educationa
importance. I have never heard any convincing denial of this state
ment. The whole secularist mindset—the self-sufficiency of the secular
—is thus entrenched in the thought of youth.

To suppose that the critics of secularism are attempting to dis-
parage the *secular* is to stand their argument on its head. The entire
drive of ethical religion is to exalt the secular to the level of a spiritual
enterprise—to overcome the dualism that isolates religion from the
common life.

I think this will be clear if attention is given to this same public

cated in such a situation is not prohibition of what the community as a whole wishes to do, but the safeguarding of the dissenting conscience from pressures and from any untoward consequence of non-conformity.

Let me here record a disclaimer which may be surprising to some of you but which is to my mind of basic importance. Again and again the question is asked of those who want to end what I may call the curricular boycott of religious subject matter, "How do you know that your proposal will make boys and girls more religious?" The right answer is, "We don't." A more adequate answer would be, "It is not the responsibility of the public schools to win their pupils to religion, but to make them intelligent about religion and the reasons why men prize it." It is the business of the schools to offer an adequate education; the cultivation of religious conviction and loyalty is the work of home and church and other non-public agencies. When we say that the school should have a positive and a reverent attitude toward religion, we mean that such an attitude is due to what is manifestly one of the most universal human concerns and has to do with what men hold sacred. The difference between such an attitude and one of evangelizing is precisely what separation of church and state means in the public classroom.

I wish now to pay my respects to the reverent exposition of Catholic convictions which go so deep as to enable a great Church to maintain a school system at immense cost, for conscience's sake. It is less than fair that the Catholic Church should have to bear the full burden of presenting a rationale for the religious day school. The National Council of Independent Schools recently issued a statement from which I think it appropriate to quote: "The independent schools are vital strongholds of religious faith in the United States. It is a cause of concern to many that in our great public school systems, with all their integrity and devotion, freedom of religion has come to mean freedom from religion. Nothing requires an independent school to make room for religion—it might theoretically devote itself to the teaching of atheism if that were what its parents and its teachers wished; but there are in fact few independent schools which do not make the inculcation of faith in God and in the brotherhood of man a guiding purpose. . . . The existence of independent schools is a major safeguard of the parent's right to see to it that his children's education includes the approach to religion which his conscience dictates." However great our devotion to the public schools, it must not be maintained at the expense of an intelligent appreciation of the purposeful non-public school.

I appreciate also the statement by one of our speakers of an official Protestant position calling for a certain measure of theological commitment on the part of the public school, a position which was definitely opposed by another Protestant educator. To my mind the issue is now between this proposal of substantive religious instruction in the schools, on the one hand, and complete negativism as to religious subject matter, on the other. The report of the American Council's Committee, *The Relation of Religion to Public Education—the Basic Principles,* which has been frequently referred to was an attempt to find a *via media.* The Educational Policies Commission of the National Education Association and the American Association of School Administrators has now come forward with substantially the same recommendation.

It is a striking coincidence indeed that the report of that Commission, *Moral and Spiritual Values in the Public Schools,* should have been made public during the final month of our Institute series. This was, for us, climactic. It is, in my judgment, much the most important document in the area of our interest here that has appeared in many years. Among its authors are President Conant of Harvard, General Eisenhower, William Jansen, superintendent of schools in New York, and Professor John K. Norton of Teachers College, Columbia University, who was then chairman of the Commission. The passage defining the place of religion in public education is so important as to warrant quoting it in full:

The public school can teach objectively *about* religion without advocating or teaching any religious creed. To omit from the classroom all references to religion and the institutions of religion is to neglect an important part of American life. Knowledge about religion is essential for a full understanding of our culture, literature, art, history, and current affairs.

That religious beliefs are controversial is not an adequate reason for excluding teaching about religion from the public schools. Economic and social questions are taught and studied in the schools on the very sensible theory that students need to know the issues being faced and to get practice in forming sound judgments. Teaching about religion should be approached in the same spirit. General guides on the teaching of all controversial issues may be helpful. If need be, teachers should be provided with special help and information to equip them to teach objectively in this area.

Although the public schools cannot teach denominational beliefs, they can and should teach much useful information about the religious faiths, the important part they have played in establishing the moral and spiritual values of American life, and their role in the story of mankind. The very fact of the variety of religions represented in this country increases the relevance of this suggestion. How many adults could state with reasonable clarity, regardless of agreement or disagreement, what the chief tenets of the various great religious faiths are? How many non-Catholics know what a Catholic believes? How many Catholics really know where Protestant views differ from their own? How much do Christians know about what Jews believe or about Jewish religious observances? What are the essential elements of the faith of Islam or of the other major creeds held by the inhabitants of this shrinking world? The unity of our own country, our understanding of the other nations of the world, and respect for the rich religious traditions of all humanity would be enhanced by instruction about religion in the public schools. Like any other teaching in which deep personal emotions are involved, such instruction should, of course, give due consideration to the varying degrees of maturity of the students.

The current facts about the churches and their influence in the United States should also be taught at appropriate points in the social studies curriculum. What, for example, are the principal religious bodies; what are the numbers of their adherents; what legal standing does religion have with respect to taxation, the courts, the Armed Forces? These are matters of obvious civic and social importance; by that token the public schools should teach about them.[4]

---

[4] James Bryant Conant, Dwight D. Eisenhower, William Jansen, John K. Norton, and others, *Moral and Spiritual Values in the Public Schools,* Educational Policies Commission of the National Education Association and the American Association of School Administrators, Washington, D.C., 1951.

To those of you who are familiar with the report of the American Council's committee the strikingly close correspondence between the recommendations in that document and what the Educational Policies Commission now puts forward will be evident. This later report has the superior merit of presenting the subject of religion in a broad context of moral and spiritual values, so that religion is seen in relation to the whole educational program. The report cuts through the fog that has enshrouded this whole matter in educational thinking. In my judgment it faces the issue reverently, realistically, and fairly.

An impressive feature of the controversy over religion in public education is the fact that in spite of sharp differences expressed in strong, sometimes indignant, words, people on opposite sides of the argument may arrive at the same substantive conclusions. Thus, Dr. Thayer, who has criticized severely the report of the American Council's committee, told us in his paper: "The school may furnish knowledge about religions as occasion arises in history, literature, social studies, science, etc., and encourage their study; but it is not the function of the public school to determine for the student the faith he should adopt." As chairman of the American Council's committee I wish to say that if there is anything in its report—or in my own writing—inconsistent with that statement, it must be due to ambiguity of phrasing. It may be, on the other hand, that the controversy has been due in no small part to the extreme difficulty people experience in accepting at face value a proposal to introduce the study of religion without sectarian bias.

Let me illustrate. When the American Council's committee was preparing its report it became apparent that some explanation must be given of what was meant by "teaching" in the context of the discussion. Then the question arose, must we not say what we mean by "religion?" The danger was obvious: any definition offered might be seized upon as a proposal to *indoctrinate for that position.* But we took the risk, offering a statement intended to include the whole range of what is commonly called religion. Sure enough, in spite of the fact that the definition of religion in that context could define nothing except *what was to be studied,* some critics took it as a proposed basis of indoctrination. Again, when we proposed that the religious phases of the various school subjects—literature, history, the arts, for example—be seriously studied and not dodged, a prominent educator declared that the proposal meant forcing religion into every school course, and sounded the tocsin! No other subject in discussion of which I have become involved is so full of hazards and so prolific of misconceptions as the one that has been engaging our attention here. But those who are really concerned about it will not be deterred on that account.

As a matter of fact, of course, the objective method contemplated by the Educational Policies Commission for studying religious institutions and practices could be carried out only by encountering them at first hand, in accord with tested methods in the social studies. The students go and see for themselves and supplement their observation by reading and discussion. This method is the expression of a great faith—the faith that what is authentic in life will disclose itself to a reverently inquiring mind.

Religion has suffered much, qualitatively speaking, in America from being divorced from the main stream of the culture as it flowed through educational channels. And the present upsurge of concern over the place of religion in the schools is evidence that the public feels that education has suffered, too. In the present state of tension harmful things might be done. One would be an attempt on the part of organized religion to dictate the program of the schools. Another would be the perpetuation in public education of a negativistic attitude toward the religious faiths of our people. I believe these addresses show the way to a constructive alternative course.

INDEX

academic freedom, *see* freedom, academic

activities, extracurricular, *see* extra-curricular activities

Adams, John, 26

Agar, Herbert, 31

Allen, Henry E., 99

Amendment, First, *see* First Amendment

American Association of Teachers Colleges, 140

American Council on Education, 30, 83, 131, 134, 138, 163

American education, *see* education, American

American life, increasing secular character of, 71

American As Reformer, The, 32

"American Tradition and the Relation between Religion and Education," 23

American Tradition in Religion and Education, 191

Aquinas, St. Thomas, 97

arts, liberal, *see* liberal arts

Atlantic Monthly, The, 97

attitude, Catholic:
    and released time plan, 63
    toward public education, 62-63

attitude, Jewish, 39-40
    historical factors in, 41-43
    religious factors in, 45-46
    social factors in, 43-45

bargaining, collective, *see* collective bargaining

Bible, 48
    power of, in a democracy, 82
    as source of religious authority, 78-79, 82

Bill of Rights, 27, 136

Bishops, Catholic, *see* Catholic Bishops

Bixler, J. Seelye, 119

Black, Hugo, Justice, 88, 105

Blanshard, Brand, 28, 29

Bowen, Catherine Drinker, 26

Boynton, Paul L., 142

Brinton, Crane, 121

Butts, R. Freeman, Professor, 191

Calvin, John, 80

capital and labor, 32

Catholic attitude, *see* attitude, Catholic

Catholic Bishops of America, 30

Catholic Bishops in the United States, 21

Catholic Philosophy of Education, A, 66

Catholic schools, *see* schools, Catholic

Christian Century, The, 15

Christian Education, 105

Christian News-Letter, 13

Christianity and democracy, 69-70

Christmas, *see* festivals, religious

church, responsibility of:
    for religious education, 91-92
    toward students, 158-159

Church of the Holy Trinity v. United States, 89

Church and State in the United States, 84, 173

Citizenship, American, Commission on, 67, 68

citizenship, education for, 61

civic unity, 73-74

civilization and religion, 162-163

Coe, George A., Dr., 15

collective bargaining, 32

colleges, American, and religious education, 19

colleges, municipal:
    intercultural education in, 113-115
    and religious activities, 113-128

205

YORK COLLEGE LIBRARY

YORK COLLEGE LIBRARY

YORK COLLEGE
Library No. 22681   26477

WESTMAR COLLEGE LIBRARY
LE MARS, IOWA